W9-BEW-141

Exposing
Witchcraft
in the Church

EXPOSING WITCHCRAFT IN THE CHURCH

RICK GODWIN

CREATION HOUSE
Orlando, FL

EXPOSING WITCHCRAFT IN THE CHURCH by Rick Godwin
Published by Creation House
Strang Communications Company
600 Rinehart Road
Lake Mary, Florida 32746
Web site: http://www.creationhouse.com

Unless otherwise noted, all Scripture quotations are from
the King James Version of the Bible.

Scripture quotations marked NIV are from the Holy Bible,
New International Version. Copyright © 1973, 1978, 1984,
International Bible Society. Used by permission.

Scripture quotations marked NAS are from the New American
Standard Bible. Copyright © 1960, 1962, 1963, 1968, 1971, 1972,
1973, 1975, 1977 by the Lockman Foundation. Used by permission.

Scripture quotations marked NKJV are from the New King James
Version of the Bible. Copyright © 1979, 1980, 1982 by Thomas
Nelson Inc., publishers. Used by permission.

Scripture quotations marked AMP are from the Amplified Bible.
Old Testament copyright © 1965, 1987 by the Zondervan
Corporation. The Amplified New Testament copyright © 1954,
1958, 1987 by the Lockman Foundation. Used by permission.

Cover Design © 1997 Jeff Haynie

Copyright © 1997 by Rick Godwin
All rights reserved
Printed in the United States of America
Library of Congress Catalog Card Number: 96-71393
ISBN: 0-88419-454-X
78901234 BBG 876543

First printing, July 1997
Second printing, September 1997

Acknowledgments

I would like to take this opportunity to thank those members of my ministry who have worked uncompromisingly to bring this important message to the attention of believers worldwide.

To Jeff Haynie, whose illustration on the cover sends shivers down one's spine.

To Mike Klassen for his excellent editorial input in the preparation of this book.

To the entire Creation House staff who have been so supportive in all aspects of this production. This has been a team effort.

To the Lord for His guidance and protection during this project.

Contents

Foreword

WITCHCRAFT IN THE CHURCH? Horrors! Impossible! "How could it be?" you ask. As I read Rick Godwin's new book, I began to see the insidious and subtle new ways that Satan uses even Spirit-filled Christians to destroy us and the church of Jesus Christ! Radical? Yes—but true! Some of those weird and far-out disturbances in our churches and in our private lives are really Satan's covert and almost imperceptible tactics that render many churches and lives powerless, ultimately destroying them.

What does cause those infamous church splits anyway? Can the Jezebel spirit actually occupy a pew? How do we identify these spirits in time and then deal with them?

Ah, dear reader, we are at war and some precious saints are stumbling around aimlessly in shell shock instead of loading up their spiritual guns with Holy Ghost bullets and putting the enemy to flight!

This book is loaded with a whole new arsenal of spiritual and practical weapons that can change your life, your church, your home, and your marriage. The victory was won at Calvary, but the war for possession of the kingdom rages on. Satan has been legally defeated, but he remains as an illegal squatter on much of what is ours by right. This book has new marching orders for us all. Let's load up in Jesus' name and dispossess the evil one's illegal entry into our God-given victory!

—Paul F. Crouch, president
Trinity Broadcasting Network

Preface

IN 1981, WHILE I WAS on the staff of Evangelist James Robison, Pastor Jim Hylton of Lake Country Baptist Church conducted a staff Bible study for us on curses and the enemy obscuring the cross. Soon after that I heard Peter Lord give further insight into the subject. I had never heard such a concept before. It radically changed my life and empowered me to walk in an authority and dimension of Christ that I had not previously known.

Later, I heard Derek Prince teach on this subject. This continued to enlarge my understanding. I was sharing this truth with all my Baptist friends, and they also were being radically changed and impacted by it.

So this book is an expansion of all the truths sown into me by many different people and from my own discoveries as I've journeyed through life. My hope is that it will profoundly affect your life (as it did mine) and dramatically improve your effectiveness as a believer and your walk with Christ.

—*Rick Godwin, pastor*
EAGLE'S NEST CHRISTIAN FELLOWSHIP
San Antonio, Texas

Introduction

- IN THE SOUTH, a pastor is murdered by a deranged member of a satanic cult. People in the community are startled by such an overt attack by someone so opposed to Christianity. Yet the news media brushed off the murder as a violent assault by a mentally disturbed if not misguided, individual.

- A once-thriving church in the Midwest slowly loses the momentum it once had, and people wonder why. After closer examination, a story emerges about a dynamic, young lady who led the women's ministry of the church. The ministry flourished, and the woman developed quite an effective prophetic ministry with a sizable share of devotees. Marriages were restored and people found their lives transformed by the power of Holy Spirit. In time, the woman began to question why the ministry was not given more exposure to the congregation.

Soon, gossip spread around the church: The young lady had "identified" spirits of control and jealousy in the senior pastor that needed to be dealt with. When the pastor challenged the lady, she pointed to his challenge as proof of his problem. Gossip, backbiting, and mistrust ran rampant throughout the congregation. People began to second-guess decisions made by the pastor and his elder board. The disagreement ended in a stalemate, and the woman left the church to start a women's ministry at another church. She left behind a congregation in the throes of division and cynicism.

- On the west coast a young, charismatic, Spirit-filled man was hired by a growing church to strengthen its evangelism and young-adult ministries. For the first few years, everything this associate pastor touched turned to gold—people were won to Christ, filled with the Holy Spirit, and the young adults became a vital part of the ministry of the church. Many people told the associate pastor that he would make a great senior pastor. Listening to the accolades of those who admired him, he began to question openly the direction in which the senior pastor was leading the church.

  When the senior pastor was forced to make the difficult decision not to pursue a building expansion project, the associate pastor informed the congregation that God brought him to that church to lead the people where the senior pastor would not and could not take them. He demanded that the senior pastor retire so that he could lead the church onward. When the demand was refused by the senior pastor, the associate resigned to start a new church, taking with him many of those whose affections he had already won. After the dust settled, a once-flourishing church had evolved into two congregations—both battered, bruised, and depleted of spiritual strength and vision.

- A charismatic church developed a reputation as a graveyard for pastors. One pastor determined not to be another casualty. In his first board meeting, he discovered an elder who wanted to wield complete control of the church ministry. Believing that God had a plan that transcended the ideas of this shortsighted elder, the pastor made a stand. People were amazed at the pastor's courage, but they ran for cover, knowing that the eventual showdown could end in a congregational free-for-all. The majority of the congregation sided with the pastor but were afraid of the power-hungry elder. Slowly the congregation dwindled in size, as those in support of the pastor grew tired of the constant push and pull. Eventually, the only people left were those in support of the elder. The pastor resigned in defeat.

- A middle-aged, divorced woman found herself unable to make a commitment to a local church. Instead, she visited any church that offered something to anesthetize her wounds. Still hurting over the rejection she faced when her husband left her, she questioned whether her husband's affair and the demise of her marriage were the result of something she had done wrong. She had given up all hope that God would or could ever use her. She read her Bible and prayed every day in hopes that she could be good enough for God to love her.

- An older man experienced a wonderful life-transforming touch from God and gave his life to Christ. He moved in a flurry of activity, and people wondered where he found his energy. Although no one could question the extent of his involvement, there seemed to be a wall that separated the real man from the man that everyone saw. He never revealed the tremendous guilt he felt for the life he had lived before he knew Christ. Every day he repented to God for what he had done in the past, yet he never felt that his confessions were quite good enough. Sadly, he never let go of the past and failed to move on with his life because of the guilt and self-condemnation he heaped upon himself. He died a sad, unhappy man who never experienced the abundant life he so desperately sought.

As you read the vignettes above, you may have been reminded of similar stories you know about which have occurred in other churches. Perhaps your church is in the middle of such a struggle. Or you may be experiencing one of these struggles yourself.

Did you know that there is a common thread interwoven into each one of these stories? How can a church split be in any way similar to a person dealing with issues of guilt? What does manipulation have to do with a low self-image? Although these examples may seem to range from one end of the spectrum to the other, each one represents the presence of witchcraft.

Witchcraft? Doesn't witchcraft have to do with spells, incantations, crystals, and the New Age movement? Yes, but witchcraft includes so much more than what the naked eye can see or the human mind can envision.

In this book you will discover Satan's strategy for defeating the church through witchcraft. The tools of his trade may include overt or subtle means, but each tool is intended to bring defeat not only to the church as a whole but to every believer.

Scripture tells us that Satan is not only a roaring lion, seeking whom he may devour, but that he is also the father of lies, and the serpent that deceived Adam and Eve (see 1 Pet. 5:8; John 8:44; Gen. 3:13). Satan is a subtle manipulator, intent on rendering the church lifeless, powerless, and impotent. Because he knows his eventual demise includes eternity in the lake of fire, he will do whatever it takes to prolong his influence in the world and on the church. Thousands, even millions of Christians go through life each day missing out on what God desires for them because they do not realize the subtle influence of witchcraft in their lives.

Countless books have been written regarding overt forms of witchcraft. Anything I would have to share about that would be treading over old territory. However, little has been written about Satan's covert operations in the church—the kind of behavior that may appear misguided but is as rooted in perversion as the most heinous of sins.

As you read this book you will discover:

- the subtle, and not so subtle, influences of

witchcraft on the church, even upon many charismatic churches.

- the relationship between guilt, condemnation, and witchcraft.

- how to spot witchcraft.

- what the living and active Word of God has to say in response to witchcraft's influence.

- how to appropriate the victory of the cross over the influences of witchcraft.

In my study of God's Word, I have discovered that the cross is the only basis of God's provision for every need of the entire human race—period.

In Revelation 2, John admonished the church in Ephesus to remember from where they had fallen and to repent. As believers who walk in the power of the Holy Spirit, we should never forget what God has brought us out of and what He has accomplished through the blood of Jesus. All too often we forget the importance and the power resident in the blood of Jesus. The purpose of this book is to help you identify the influences of witchcraft in your life and to learn how to appropriate the power of the cross to overcome these influences.

May God bless you as you read, and may He give you eyes to see and ears to hear what the "Spirit says to the churches" (Rev. 2:7, NKJV).

Part 1

BEWITCHED,
BE-WONDERED,
AND BEWILDERED

One

THE ESSENCE OF WITCHCRAFT

HAT YOU ARE ABOUT TO READ affects every person you know, including you. Chances are you have dealt with it knowingly or unknowingly. When most people see the word *witchcraft,* they automatically expect to see its more obvious manifestations. Witchcraft can take on the appearance of overt manifestations, but it also can take on a much more subtle, more discreet demeanor.

In this chapter we will take an overall look at the essence of witchcraft. You will discover that legalism, trusting in the flesh, manipulation, intimidation, and domination all have their roots in the same source. To start, let's take a look at some of witchcraft's more overt forms.

1

Witchcraft, Divination, and Sorcery

There are three main English words we use for the study of witchcraft—witchcraft, divination, and sorcery. Most versions and translations of Scripture use these three words interchangeably. Basically, witchcraft is satanic power. It is Satan's way of imposing his will on your will and imposing emotions, behaviors, or circumstances on people they would not otherwise want. Witchcraft imposes its power primarily through curses and spells.

Divination is fortune-telling. Predicting the future is a significant way by which Satan drags people into his net because there is a tremendous, insatiable desire to know the future. Divination can also be found in the church—sometimes masquerading as prophecy.

Sorcery is that which operates through objects. These objects which become a means through which the supernatural power of Satan is released. Amulets, charms, fetishes, potions, things you drink, and drugs can be counted as sorcery. At times music can also fit this category.

The Root Is the Key to the Fruit

Problems that affect people can be likened to a tree. On a tree's outermost regions are its branches which are connected to the main trunk. The trunk is supported firmly beneath the soil by roots. If anything happens to the root system, the whole tree is affected. Let's look at an example of how people's problems are a result of "affected roots."

Betty and Jane shared common circumstances—both were married to husbands who were unfaithful. The men spent more money than they earned, and neither of them honored their wives with dignity and respect.

The wives, in turn, searched for an outlet to deal with their rejection: Betty was a member of a church that found social drinking acceptable, and she wound up an alcoholic; Jane was a member of a church that forbids drinking, so she swapped a burger for a bottle, becoming a foodaholic. Thus both women's overindulgence led to addiction, covering up the root problem—rejection.

Do you see the connection? Neither woman will be helped by dealing solely with the addiction. Their addiction is a branch that grew out of their rejection. The addiction is not the *source* of the problem; it is a problem, but it's not the root. It's like cutting a branch or pulling a leaf off the tree. Branches and leaves grow back. If you treat only the addiction, it will come back. The problem must be dealt with at the root. The problem goes beyond the addictions for both women— it goes all the way to the responses they give to their dysfunctional husbands. A key to their recovery will be their decision to forgive their husbands and lay down their bitterness, resentment, and judgment. Lacking forgiveness, they will never go free. They may get a temporary fix, but the addiction will come right back. Perhaps it will even be worse.

WITCHCRAFT: THE ROOT OF ALL REBELLION

WHEN YOU TREAT THE ROOT OF THE TREE, you treat the fruit. So what is the root? *Rebellion.* It always is. It is the root of all human problems, and its roots run deepest.

Through Samuel the prophet God instructed King Saul to attack and utterly destroy the Amalekites for opposing the children of Israel when they first arrived in the Promised Land generations before (see 1 Sam. 15). Not just the men were to be destroyed but all the women, children, babies, and cattle—everything! King

3

Saul, as instructed, conquered the Amalekites, but he failed to follow through with God's directives. He destroyed all the people and animals but reserved the choicest livestock for his men and himself. He also preserved the life of Agag, king of the Amalekites. When Samuel confronted Saul for failing to obey God's commands completely, he rebuked Saul by saying, "For rebellion is as the sin of witchcraft, and stubbornness is as iniquity and idolatry" (1 Sam. 15:23, NKJV).

You don't have to participate in a séance to be dabbling in witchcraft. Notice two things about that scripture: *Rebellion* is likened to *witchcraft;* and stubbornness is likened to idolatry. That's how God views these two things. Rebellion is witchcraft. A spirit is behind rebellion, and it's not the Holy Spirit. Rebellion says, "I will not do it. *I won't.*"

STUBBORNNESS IS IDOLATRY

STUBBORNNESS IS CALLED *IDOLATRY.* How can a stubborn person be in idolatry? He makes an idol of all his opinions. His opinions become gods to him. In the church we expound our pet doctrines and pet interpretations of vague doctrines, becoming stubborn and immovable from them. Stubbornness says, "I'll do it *my way.*" God calls this *idolatry.* We might just as well bow down and worship an idol because that is what we are doing. And the pity is, the pet teaching we are worshiping may not even be true! That's dangerous. Such idolatry takes place in the church and in the pew every single day.

REBELLION IS WITCHCRAFT

REBELLION IS LIKENED TO THE SIN of witchcraft. Rebellion and witchcraft are as alike as identical twin sisters. In the ministry of deliverance, if you find one, you'd better

4

look for the other one. If witchcraft is there, so is rebellion. If rebellion is there, look for witchcraft. They are seldom separated. In the New Testament witchcraft is described in two ways—first, as a work of the flesh; second, as an evil, spiritual power. We see the effect of this evil, spiritual power in Galatians 3:1. Paul says, "[Who] has bewitched you that you should not obey the truth, before whose eyes Jesus Christ was clearly portrayed among you as crucified?" (NKJV). An evil spiritual power had come upon the Galatians blinding them to the work of the cross. They started trusting in their Jewishness and circumcision instead of experiencing the grace that comes by trusting Jesus Christ.

In Galatians 5:19–20, Paul includes witchcraft and idolatry as works of the flesh along with adultery, fornication, hatred, murder, and drunkenness. Such fleshly works are the behaviors of unregenerate, fallen humanity. Rebellion is a work of the flesh because it is the rejection of God's legitimate authority.

The ruler who does not rule under the authority of God is an illegitimate ruler, and he uses illegitimate power to enforce his rule. His illegitimate power is witchcraft. That is why rebellion and witchcraft are twins. The essence of rebellion is the rejection of the righteous, legal, legitimate government of God in one's life, church, or anywhere. In order to keep things orderly, some kind of rule or government must be invoked over people. If that rule, government, or ruler is not submitted to the righteous government of God, it is an evil, illegitimate government. The means of power it uses to enforce its government is called witchcraft. As we just studied, witchcraft is a work of the flesh, and all believers can be exposed to it.

In God's original plan for mankind, before the Fall, man was given a mandate: to subdue and take dominion over all the earth (see Gen. 1). God purposed for man to rule under His authority as His representative, or God's ambassador, on the earth. Thus part of man's deepest inherent inclination is to rule.

In the Garden, Adam rejected and rebelled against God's legitimate authority and became a rebel. Even today, as successors to the first Adam, men still have within them the innate desire to subdue and have dominion. It makes no difference whether you are a believer or an unbeliever, if you are a man, you still have the desire for rulership within you because it was planted by God in your first father, Adam.

If that desire to subdue and have dominion is expressed in a fleshly, illegitimate way, it is an expression of witchcraft. It becomes illegitimate when the person in control attempts to coerce or manipulate people to do what they otherwise would not do. When you discover the essence of witchcraft, you find it is amazingly common as well as frightening. You will find it on TV, hear in the pulpit, and observe it in the business world. You may even find it in your own relationship with your spouse or children. In the next chapter we are going to take a closer look at how witchcraft expresses itself in the home.

IDENTIFYING WITCHCRAFT

THERE ARE THREE KEY WORDS that act as caution flags in identifying witchcraft: *manipulation, domination,* and *intimidation.* Whenever you run into these three things, an evil spirit lurks not far behind. This is the devil's *modus operandi.* God never manipulates, God never dominates, and God never intimidates. But Satan takes authority by using illegitimate means because his authority has been stripped from him by God. In the same manner, since I am born of the first Adam—even if I am born again—that old man in me still wants to "do it my way" and be in complete control. It may be in a church, a board of elders, a marriage, or a business— it doesn't matter. When someone asserts authority not given by God it is called witchcraft; it is rebellion against delegated, legitimate authority. With such illegitimate authority, one resorts to manipulating, dominating, or intimidating in order to rule over other people.

Let's now take a closer look at how witchcraft rears its ugly head in the family and within the family of God.

Two

WITCHCRAFT IN THE FAMILY

THE CHILD SEEMED TO PERSONIFY the poem about the little girl with the curl on her forehead: When she was good she was very, very good, but when she was bad, she was horrid. Four-year-old Cherie was cute as a button and could turn on the charm like nobody's business. But one Sunday after church when Cherie's parents told her it was time to go home, she turned horrid. "I *hate* you Mommy and Daddy! You never let me do what *I* want to do! I hate you!" Cherie screamed.

"Now, honey," her mother pleaded, "we told you five minutes ago that we would have to leave in just a little bit. It's time to go home."

"I won't go home! I want to play!" Cherie retorted and off she ran to play with her friends. The barrage of

9

emotion took the once-charmed bystanders by surprise. No one knew *how* to respond—including her parents.

The response of her parents astonished those in attendance even further. "Well," Cherie's mother offered to the people standing around, "I guess we'll let her play just a little bit longer." The family finally left for their home *when Cherie was ready.*

If you had been a bystander to the aforementioned episode, would you be surprised to be told that you had just witnessed the presence of witchcraft? Please understand that I am not saying every child who exhibits behavior like this is possessed by some sort of demon. What I *am* saying is that conduct such as this child's manipulative behavior has roots in witchcraft akin to what was explained in the previous chapter.

In the last chapter we looked at the essence of witchcraft. Witchcraft, in its most subtle form affects every person, every church, and every family. Many problems in family relationships can be traced to roots of witchcraft. Discovering and identifying the root is a key to dealing with the resultant fruit. The deepest root of all is rebellion. Rebellion is the use of illegitimate, ill-gotten authority, and it expresses itself through manipulation, intimidation, and domination.

In this chapter we are going to study how to identify witchcraft in the family. You will see how manipulation, domination, and intimidation express themselves not only among children but in husbands and wives as well. Although the purpose of this book is to expose witchcraft in the church, most often witchcraft in the above forms begins and is fostered in the family. Once witchcraft takes root, it affects every area of a person's life. And it eventually finds its way into the church.

Witchcraft in the Family

THE PARENTS' AUTHORITY

TO UNDERSTAND THE EFFECTS of witchcraft in family relationships, it is vital that we begin with the Word of God. The Bible teaches us that God has placed parents in authority over their children (see Eph. 6:1–2). It may be contested in the courts, but it's not contested in the Word of God. Parents, did you know that your children are under your authority? The fifth commandment in Deuteronomy 5 says: "Honor your father and your mother, as the Lord your God has commanded you, that your days may be long, and that it may be well with you in the land which the Lord your God is giving you" (v. 16, NKJV).

God called every child to honor his or her father and mother. The Hebrew word for *honor—kabad—*also means "to glorify." This is the same term used for glorifying God. Giving honor or glory means showing that person respect, attention, and obedience. When we honor our parents, we are, in fact, honoring God. Because God has placed our parents in authority over us, as we honor them, we honor God.

The parent must govern the child. If the child instead governs the parent, that child is exercising illegitimate authority. As we already know, illegitimate authority is witchcraft.

MANIPULATION IN THE FAMILY

CHILDREN ARE EXPERTS AT MANIPULATION. In the example you just read, young Cherie exhibited quite an unhealthy dose of manipulation. She knew that if she made a big enough scene in front of those around, her browbeaten parents would give in. That cute little girl resorted to the use of an illegitimate authority called witchcraft to get her way.

11

Cherie's parents are more to blame for the behavior she exhibited than Cherie is. Had corrective discipline been dealt swiftly and decisively, the behavior could have been nipped in the bud before it became a habitual problem. If her parents don't put a stop to it, young Cherie will go through life—perhaps even the Spirit-filled Christian life—as a master manipulator.

Children can be just as skilled at working one parent against the other. "Mom?" little Billy asks one Saturday morning, "Can I go over to Eddie's house to play?"

"No, we have to get your hair cut," mother replies. But Billy *really* wants to play Eddie's new video game, so he goes to his father. "Dad, can I go over to Eddie's house to play?"

Not being aware of the earlier exchange between Billy and his mother, he gives Billy permission.

As Billy walks out the door, his mom asks where he is going. *"Dad* said I could go over to Eddie's house to play."

Dad enters the scene. "Honey, you can take Billy to get his hair cut later; Eddie's going to be gone this afternoon." Soon Mom and Dad are experiencing some intense fellowship as they go back and forth deciding whether Billy can go over to Eddie's.

Now what has that child just done? Manipulated both parents. He's manipulated the authority delegated by God over him through illegitimate means. What's making him do it? The desire to get his own way. He wants *control.* What's the root of his behavior? *Rebellion.*

Manipulative children who continue in their manipulative ways grow into manipulative adults. In marriage, they are much more cunning than their children or, perhaps, their spouses. Take Jack and Sheila for example.

Jack eyes an expensive power tool that will top off his master power-tool collection and put him in the same category as Tim the Tool-man. It's an expense he knows would stretch the family budget way beyond reason. Apart from the budget, the other obstacle is his wife, Sheila—she runs the budget. Together they have decided not to make any major purchases unless both are in agreement. Hence, the prospects for his purchase are slim to none.

Suddenly an opportunity for control emerges—when Sheila mentions that she needs to go to the mall, she is somewhat surprised when Jack asks to go along. Once at the mall, the cunning Jack eyes a pretty dress. "Sheila, look at this beautiful dress. Why don't you try it on?" With minimal coaxing, she relents. When she models it for him, he goes nuts. Naturally, it looks absolutely stunning on her. "Just this once," he offers, "let's splurge a little."

"How can I say no to common sense?" she answers back.

The next day, Jack moves in for the kill: "Hey Sheila, I happened to be reading the paper today, and I noticed that the Black and Decker Power Saw 1000 is on sale. If I had it, I could make that playhouse for the kids."

"Jack," Sheila replies, "we just bought me a new dress . . . " but she stops mid-sentence. Both realize, of course, that he just won the round. If they spent their money on a dress for her, it would only be fair to purchase the power tool for him.

The list goes on and on. A wife can play the master-manipulation game just as well as a husband. Sadly, such behavior flourishes in Christian marriages. Countless people have grown up believing behavior such as this is normal.

How do we manipulate? We use weapons like guilt and fear. Adult children stay at home, living off their parents, threatening that if they can't live their own way they'll move out and live on the streets. We remind our spouse of what he or she did to us twenty years ago. We use threats like, "If you don't do this, I'll leave you and take the children." We use sex as a tool to get our own way. Are these manipulations done in the power of the Holy Ghost? Absolutely not! They are nothing more than a spirit of witchcraft—illegitimate authority.

DOMINATION IN THE FAMILY

DOMINATION IS ONE STEP past manipulation. Manipulation is *covert,* while domination is *overt* in nature. Manipulation says, "I'll *trick* you into doing things my way." Domination says, "I'll *make* you do things my way."

Sometimes a child is discouraged from growing independent and leaving the nest when he becomes an adult. John was fifty-five years old and had always lived with his mother. His father deserted the family when John was a child, and his mother never remarried. Wielding guilt, condemnation, and threats of rejection as tools of control, John's mother convinced him that if he were to ever leave her, even to get married, he would be abandoning her just like her husband did. John decided to forego developing any romantic relationships for fear that his mother would feel threatened. Soon after she died, John married and became as domineering a husband as his mother had been to him. Once browbeaten himself, now his thirst for control and incessant barbs of guilt formed a wedge between his wife and him.

Not at all encouraged by the prospects of spending the rest of her life with an immature, domineering husband, she divorced him. Consequently, John died a lonely, disillusioned man. The root of the problem? Witchcraft. The thief came and stole that man's life. The dominating spirit of witchcraft which was present in John's mother had been passed to the next generation.

His mother exerted an illegitimate authority over her son and he in turn tried it on another.

Scripture gives us numerous examples of sins that are passed on from one generation to the next. An example of generational domination can be seen in the family of Jezebel, the evil queen who reigned with her husband, Ahab (see 1 Kings 16–18).

Jezebel was a tyrant who corrupted her husband, as well as the nation of Israel, by promoting pagan worship. When she married Ahab, she decided to turn the city of Jezreel into a city that worshiped Baal, a Phoenician god. The wicked, idolatrous queen soon became the power behind the throne. After Ahab's death, Jezebel's son, Ahaziah, became king.

Ahaziah continued the domination his mother had wielded through policies he established. Though he only reigned for two years, the nation of Israel was held captive to his domination and manipulation (see 1 Kings 22). But the spirit of domination in Ahaziah had not begun with Jezebel. Scripture records that at the time of Ahaziah's ascent to the throne, Mesha, the king of Moab, rebelled against his rulership because Mesha had already suffered from the manipulative domination of Ahaziah's grandfather, Omri, the father of Ahab (see 2 Kings 1–3). The spirit of domination which had clutched at the grandfather had also found a resting spot in the grandson.[1]

Sadly enough, parental domination is rampant among Christian families! Under the guise of honoring our father and mother, men and women allow themselves to be absorbed by a domineering parent. We owe our parents honor, but it should never interfere with "leaving and cleaving." In Genesis 2:24, when God commanded man to leave his father and mother and cleave to his wife, God released the husband and wife from the authority of their parents. If a parent still tries to control the lives of their children after they are married, they are operating in domination.

Domineering husbands can do the same thing with their wives. Over time, a wife may become completely absorbed into the personality of her husband. Often this absorption occurs after years of manipulation as the husband fights for control in the relationship. When a husband isolates his wife from other people, not permitting her to have relationships outside the home, that's control. When a wife stays at home to raise the kids while the husband insists on deciding for himself how the finances will be spent because *he* is the breadwinner, that's control.

People who are driven by control and domination have difficulty submitting themselves under the authority of Jesus Christ. The need for control is just a variation of rebellion. Control says, "I want to be in charge." Domination tricks, or coerces, people into doing something they *do not* want to do. Control restricts the person from doing what they *do* want to do. Either action is a form of witchcraft which is rooted in rebellion and illegitimate authority.

The apostle Paul writes, "Stand fast therefore in the liberty by which Christ has made us free, and do not be entangled again with a yoke of bondage" (Gal. 5:1, NKJV). Christ has set us free, and we have no business bringing people back under bondage or placing ourselves under bondage either.

INTIMIDATION IN THE FAMILY

ONE STEP PAST DOMINATION is intimidation. Intimidation says, "I'll scare you into doing things my way." Intimidation rules by fear—fear of punishment. What does the Bible say about fear and punishment? "There is no fear in love. But perfect love drives out fear, because fear has to do with punishment. The man who fears is not made perfect in love" (1 John 4:18, NIV). Love and fear are opposing forces. Because love flourishes in an atmosphere of mutual affection and acceptance, both parties are intrinsically motivated to remain in the relationship. But intimidation operates from fear on both sides: Fear on the part of the perpetrator that he or she will lose what they already have, including the person under their control; and fear of possible further punishment on the part of the recipient. Anytime a parent rules with fear, he or she is ruling in witchcraft—not in love. Remember what witchcraft is? It's *making* people do things that you want them to do.

So how do we intimidate another? An extreme example would be child or spousal abuse. We can shake our heads about how destructive abuse is, but it happens in Christian families as well as in the world. We cannot forget that, to the child, we represent God. When overbearing parents intimidate their children in the name of God, those children view God as a harsh taskmaster—just the way they view their parents. When we rule by intimidation, we teach our children that God rules by intimidation. Yet just who is it that rules by intimidation? Satan.

Sometimes it seems that God trusts us more than we trust others. God gave us the decision to choose or reject Jesus Christ. On the other hand, we like to control not only our destiny but often the destinies of others as well.

Every time I insist on having my own way I expose myself to satanic, demonic influence. Every time. The door just swings wide open, and Satan's hosts can come right in. If I don't submit to God's righteous authority, to His plan, and to His way, I'll reach out through manipulation, domination, or intimidation—witchcraft—to get my way.

Witchcraft takes many forms in family relationships. Perhaps this chapter will enlighten you to some of its various forms so that you will be able to better identify it in the future. You may even see how it has taken root in your own life. As you continue through this book you will discover that Jesus has already delivered you from the powers of rebellion and witchcraft. Satan's plan of attack against the believer is to make the power of the cross obscure.

Thanks be to God that no family is without hope. God gave us a tremendous promise in Philippians 1:6: "He who has begun a good work in you will complete it until the day of Jesus Christ" (NKJV). Eventually Cherie's parents learned how to deal with their daughter in a healthy, balanced way that was neither manipulative, dominating, nor abusive. That day at church when Cherie threw such an unforgettable tirade proved to be a watershed event for her parents. The process toward a healthy family, free from the influence of witchcraft, however, required intestinal fortitude, consistency, prayer, and good old-fashioned hard work. The time Cherie's family spent in counseling with two godly, experienced, retired parents made the difference between a child being raised to be domineering and manipulative and a child who was raised in the fear and admonition of the Lord. Today, Cherie has children of her own. This time, however, she can fall back on the knowledge borne out of her own experience from her childhood years. Fortunately, her parents were alert enough to identify their own weaknesses and seek help from the right places.

Now that we've taken a brief overview of witchcraft in the family, let's see how it takes root in the family of God.

Three

Manipulation,
Thy Name Is Jezebel

THE FAMILY UNIT IS A PROTOTYPE of the local church. Families are made of persons interconnected by a common bond of blood relationship. In a similar way, churches are made of people united in a common bond through the blood of Jesus. It is no mistake that the apostle Paul refers to the body of believers as the household of faith (Gal. 6:10). Above all, churches, as well as families, contain people with very real shortcomings. Dysfunctions inherent within a family eventually surface in the body of Christ.

Countless churches around the world stagger under the weight of their walking wounded. Held captive to the control of a few, these churches resemble a barren wasteland of spiritual bodies scattered over the battlefields of dissension and manipulation. Unless strong leadership is in place, a single person can render a church defenseless—even in Spirit-filled congregations! Casualties mount as people, disillusioned with the faith, find their message rendered impotent; their testimony, powerless.

In this chapter and the next we will confront two spiritual forces—Jezebel and Lucifer. You will learn to identify the presence of Jezebel and Lucifer in your church. Jezebel is primarily attracted to the prophetic personalities; Lucifer is attracted to strong charismatic, Pentecostal, faith, and evangelical churches. Jezebel is exhibited more often in the female gender, although males can also exhibit the same spirit. Lucifer is exhibited predominately in males. As we have already learned, the root of witchcraft is rebellion, which expresses itself through manipulation, domination, and intimidation. Often the three are so intermingled in the spirits of Jezebel and Lucifer that they are difficult to distinguish.

JEZEBEL AND LUCIFER: AN ANSWER TO PRAYER

THESE TWO SPIRITS ARE TOXIC to the church and often most difficult to detect in the early stages. They can hide in anointed, gifted, hard-working, friendly people who seem to be an answer to prayer. Initially when such a person appears in your church you are very excited. They seem to have such high-level potential for ministry. But when you strip away the veneer, underneath lies rebellion, accusation, manipulation, control, lying, anger, arrogance, super-spirituality, rumor-spreading, criticism, jealousy, cunning, craftiness, and false concern.

> Notwithstanding I have a few things against thee, because thou sufferest that woman Jezebel, which calleth herself a prophetess, to teach and to

seduce my servants to commit fornication, and to eat things sacrificed unto idols. And I gave her space to repent of her fornication; and she repented not. Behold, I will cast her into a bed, and them that commit adultery with her into great tribulation, except they repent of their deeds. And I will kill her children with death; and all the churches shall know that I am he which searcheth the reins and hearts: and I will give unto every one of you according to your works.

—Revelation 2:20–23

At first glance, it may appear that there isn't a modern-day equivalent for the Jezebel of Revelation 2. Yet many church members—even many pastors—have succumbed to the alluring temptress spirit of Jezebel. Lured into a snare of adultery and fornication, and sacrificing holiness to the idol of sexual immorality, they have entered a period of great tribulation. Homes and churches have been wrecked, and many children, both physical and spiritual, have suffered a form of death.

THE NATURE OF JEZEBEL

IN THE BOOK OF REVELATION, the Holy Spirit spoke through the apostle John to seven churches in the Roman province of Asia. One of the churches, located in Thyatira, was dealing with a Jezebel spirit. In the Old Covenant, Jezebel was a living, breathing woman; but in the New Covenant she is a spirit. In the same way, Old Testament Babylon was a literal place; in the New Testament, Babylon is a spirit, not limited to a specific location. Often that which is singular and local in the Old Testament is corporate, boundless, and spiritual in the New Testament. This is significant because when you are dealing with Jezebel, you are dealing with a

21

spirit more than you are dealing with flesh and blood.

Jezebel's involvement in Scripture does not begin in Revelation but goes back 950 years earlier to the time of King Ahab. Let's review who Jezebel was.

In 1 Kings 16, Ahab, king of Israel took Jezebel to be his wife. Jezebel was not from Israel; she was the daughter of the king of Sidon. Even worse, she was a very evangelistic and devoted worshiper of Baal. Ahab, the weak-kneed king that he was, also began worshiping Baal. Together they led Israel into the sin of idol worship. God in His anger raised up Elijah to call Israel to repentance and to speak a famine over the land.

Then in 1 Kings, chapter 18, Jezebel killed the prophets of God. She usurped an authority God did not give her, and she killed people God had raised up to be His anointed mouthpiece. In their stead, she replaced them with the prophets of Baal. Responding to her wickedness, God sent Elijah to confront the powers of Baal in a show of force before the people of Israel. With the prophets of Baal on one side of the mountain and Elijah on the other, God demonstrated before the children of Israel that the God of Elijah was the one true God. As fire from heaven struck the altar Elijah constructed, the people fell on their faces chanting, "The Lord, he is the God; the Lord, he is the God" (1 Kings 18:39). Elijah commanded all those around to slay the prophets of Baal, and the people quickly obliged. Within twenty-four hours, the famine was broken as a revival began to spread throughout Israel.

When Ahab reported to Jezebel what God had done through Elijah, she sent a message back to her adversary: "Let the gods do to me, and more also, if I make not thy life as the life of one of them by tomorrow about this time" (1 Kings 19:2). Unaffected by the mighty demonstration of power by the God of Israel, Jezebel came after God's anointed prophet.

Wait a minute: Where was Ahab? *Who* was the king in Israel? Jezebel wasn't king—Ahab was. But it sure didn't look like it! Jezebel was running the show. Operating from behind the scenes through her spineless husband, she used manipulation, intimidation, and domination to assert her illegitimate rule through witchcraft.

That's why Jezebel is so dangerous. She hungers for control, and she'll use any means at her disposal in order to secure it.

In 1 Kings, chapter 21, Ahab eyed a vineyard in Jezreel that would make a lovely addition to the palace garden. Unfortunately, its owner, Naboth, refused to sell it to him. So what did Jezebel do? She directed the elders and nobles of Jezreel to frame Naboth for the crime of blaspheming God. In the end, Naboth was stoned to death so Jezebel could acquire the garden for her husband. Worst of all, the leadership of Israel complied with Jezebel's directive. Why? Because they were afraid of Jezebel—just as Elijah was. People looked at Jezebel and said, "That is one person you do *not* want to mess with." The irony is that Jezebel framed Naboth for speaking against the one true God of Israel, while at the same time she was trying to draw Israel into *Baal* worship. Jezebel can be blatant and manipulative at the same time.

We wrestle with the same problem in evangelical churches. The man behind the pulpit is often not in charge. Some person, a woman or a man on the deacon board or in the laity, may be running the church by witchcraft.

Denominations can use witchcraft by saying or intimating, "If you don't believe and say everything we tell you to say . . . if you have that person speak . . . we'll cut you off and take your credentials." That's nothing less than control through intimidation.

The Jezebel Spirit

In Hebrew *Jezebel* means both "Baal is husband" and "inability to cohabitate." Jezebel refuses to partner with anyone because she is allied to Baal, a false lord. She wears the pants; she leads, she controls, she rules. She shares nothing with no one.

In the example of the church in Thyatira, it was Jezebel's claim—not that of the people of the church in Thyatira—that she is a prophetess:

> Notwithstanding I have a few things against thee, because thou sufferest that woman Jezebel, *which calleth herself a prophetess,* to teach and to seduce my servants to commit fornication, and to eat things sacrificed unto idols.
> —Revelation 2:20, italics added

The fornication into which she is seducing the faithful in Christ can be literal, sexual, or spiritual. The people in the Thyatiran church were either seduced by her persona, or fearful of her manipulative personality—or both.

Jezebel's Agenda

So what is Jezebel's agenda? False religion, false doctrine, and most of all, the undermining of authority. Anywhere you find a Jezebel you will likely find weak men with passive authority. A Jezebel spirit feeds on Ahabs—weak men, men-fearers, and men-pleasers. She goes after leadership with the intent of rendering it useless, powerless, and lifeless. Using any means necessary, she lures people away from a true spiritual covering—from their pastor and from their church—and entices them into her sphere of influence. The tools of her trade can range from false prophecy to flattery and even sex. She fiercely defends her little kingdom and fosters unusual dependence from her followers. Her groups are literally covens of witchcraft, but of course the Jezebel spirit would never reveal that overtly, so the covens are often referred to as home groups or Bible study groups.

Above all, a person exhibiting a Jezebel spirit resents strong male leadership. Often her repulsion results from a dysfunctional relationship with her physical father. The father may have been absent, or he may have been physically or sexually abusive. Although never justified, it explains how she became so resentful.

Troubled by the helpless feelings of her past, she yearns to control her environment. Her Bible study group presents a platform for undermining the leadership of her church. Even her prayers seem to resound with the resentment she feels toward those in leadership: "Father, show our pastor the deeper things You're revealing to us." She is committing *sedition*—"the undermining of God-delegated, constituted authority with the intent to overthrow." We use another word for it—*treason.*

In a nation, it is punishable by death. People who commit sedition will never say, "I'm here to undermine your leadership." Neither does Satan wave his arms, telling the Christian where he is and what he plans to do. Galatians 5:20 lists *sedition* as a work of the flesh. Therefore, people that participate in this sin will not inherit the kingdom of God.

The subtle, stealth-like attack upon the church through sedition has caused many church splits. It has destroyed relationships, created dissension, and fueled the fight in church wars. Any attempt to undermine the spiritual authority of church leaders is sedition.

Jezebel is an expert at undermining leaders' authority.

Jezebel drives God's anointed leaders to discouragement, despair, suicide, and even depression just as she did the prophet Elijah. After Elijah called fire down from heaven and ordered the Israelites to slay the false prophets of Baal, Jezebel decided to go after him. Here was an anointed prophet, running for his life, beseeching God, "Lord, kill me. I am the only one left; just kill me." Many leaders encounter deep periods of loneliness and discouragement during which they despair of life. They may never share their feelings even with their wives or closest friends. Unbeknown to them, they may be dealing with a powerful Jezebel spirit that seeks to dominate and control.

Before Satan comes after the sheep, he first comes after the shepherd. Then he gets the sheep. Zechariah 13:7 says, "Smite the shepherd, and the sheep shall be scattered." Leaders bear the impact of Satan's attack before the rest of the body does; because when the leaders fall, the sheep are scattered! That's exactly what Satan wants. He'll take one leader for a thousand sheep. This is why Paul admonished the church to pray regularly and fervently for those in authority.

> I exhort therefore, that, first of all, supplications, prayers, intercessions, and giving of thanks, be made for . . . kings, and for all that are in authority.
> —1 Timothy 2:1–2

Those in authority come under attack due to the nature of the position they hold.

Not long ago, I received word about a pastor who spent thirty years in one city building a church of three or four thousand people. One day he walked out of the house, left town, and faxed his wife for a divorce after thirty years of marriage. She had no idea anything was even wrong. Now, people can say, "Oh, what a

26

wicked. . . . " Hold it! Thirty years invested in the kingdom of God; thirty years with one woman, no adultery, no immorality, no lack of integrity; great church—what happened? Jezebel happened!

Both Jezebel and Lucifer cause church splits, broken marriages, and destroyed lives. We should not cast these casualties out of our fellowships; instead we should go after them and seek to bring them back to God. Such a man can be rescued, delivered, and saved before he incurs the wrath of God. But under the control of Jezebel, he doesn't *know* he can be redeemed, and so he despairs and does foolish things. Worst of all, the rest of the body judges him without even knowing the details.

DYSFUNCTIONAL, DEFENSIVE, AND NOSY

MORE TIMES THAN NOT, a person with a Jezebel spirit comes from a dysfunctional family background. Jezebel feeds on dysfunction. Usually in the family history one can find alcoholism, abuse, mental illness, parental domination, or some other sort of dysfunction. It is not uncommon for Jezebel to be sexually unclean or to have some other sexual perversion in her life. Because she is dysfunctional, dysfunctional people are attracted to her. But beneath the seedy veneer lies a person with deep hurts and wounds.

When she is challenged, Jezebel becomes defensive and reacts with hostility. She lashes back with guilt-ridden accusations such as, "You're not praying enough. You're not submitted to authority. You're in rebellion. How could you do this to me? I love you! I've given you my life!" With aggression, she will intimidate, quote Scripture, and try to make those who challenge her feel inferior. She is skilled at talking people out of challenging her seditious ways, but when they walk away they feel dirty because they know they have been used.

Another characteristic of the Jezebel spirit is that she must know everything going on in the church—from top to bottom. She is very nosy and thrives on information. Because she wants to know about everybody—their ministry, their marriage, their children, their jobs, their problems—she concerns herself with church matters that are none of her business.

At times it may be difficult to detect the spirit of Jezebel at work in a church. She may masquerade as care, concern, intercession, support, or a number of other positive characteristics. Jezebel is a master at disguising her tactics.

Gossip is one of the biggest threats to the spiritual life of any church. The old "Christian grapevine" is a favorite tool used by Jezebel. The sins and failures of many church members easily become common knowledge at the church prayer meeting: "Let's pray for Brother So-and-So; he's been seen doing such-and-such" or "Let's intercede for Brother and Sister Marriage-In-A-Jam, they are having troubles again." I can just see the smirk on Jezebel's face as her influence lands right on the noses of these "intercessors."

DEALING WITH JEZEBEL

JEZEBEL, WITH HER EVIL SCHEMES and tactics, will have a toxic affect upon the church if she is not dealt with swiftly and thoroughly. There are two methods of dealing with Jezebel which will stop her influence and expel her from your midst.

1. *Confront Jezebel head-on, using strong spiritual authority to rid yourself—and your church—of her influence.*

We cannot sit idly by, watching Jezebel at work in our churches and in the lives of our friends and fellow believers, wishing she would just go away. Her intent is to undermine the spiritual authority God has given to the leaders He has placed over a church, and she will stop at nothing in order to get her way. Stand up to her, confront her sin, render it useless with the authority God has given to you, and stop her influence in your midst.

> *2. Live in submission to God, and teach those under your spiritual authority to live in submission also.*

Submission is the solution to sedition. When a woman is submitted to her husband, Jezebel's tactics cannot affect that marriage. When a man is submitted to the leadership of his church, he will not undermine that authority with seditious words and behaviors. When a body of believers is submitted to its leaders, that church will grow and develop into a beacon of light in the dark, sinful world around it.

Like any label, the term *Jezebel* is easy to apply to situations or persons but not so easy to remove. In his book *Growing in the Prophetic,* Mike Bickle urges those in authority to beware of hastily throwing around labels such as Jezebel. He writes, "Too many women who have a leadership gift are labeled Jezebels simply because they clash with a man who has a controlling personality."[1] Sadly, many of us respond to others out of our own insecurities. When we do, casualties are not far behind.

At the end of the next chapter, you will learn how to deal further with Jezebel and with her partner in crime—Lucifer.

Four

LUCIFER: AMBITION TO POSITION

JOHN WAS THE KIND OF ASSOCIATE every senior pastor dreamed of: He was an empathetic counselor, his enthusiasm drew people into whatever project he was working on, and above all, he seemed to complement Pastor Henry's weaknesses. Their relationship personified that of Elijah and Elisha. As the church grew, many in the congregation anticipated a bright future for their church. Twenty-five years his senior, Pastor Henry had mentored John as a college student and, after graduation, brought him on the church staff. Now, eight years later, there were as many people attending the church who were a product of John's ministry as of Pastor Henry's.

Soon, due to the rapid growth of their church, another associate was brought on staff. Charles was not only gifted with youth, but he was also a fiery preacher. Making room for Charles would mean less time "up front" for John when Pastor Henry was out of town for his many speaking engagements. As Pastor Henry developed the new associate's job description, John confronted him. "Hank, am I to assume that by bringing Charles on staff, I am going to be preaching less?"

Taken aback by his forthrightness, Pastor Henry replied, "Yes, you'll probably be speaking less, but I thought this would be a good chance for you to focus on developing our cell-group ministry."

"Why didn't you give him the cell groups and let me continue preaching?" John retorted.

"Because I'm trying to play to our strengths," Henry answered.

"Are you saying you think Charles is a better preacher than me?" John said defensively.

"No, that's not what I said," Henry quickly responded. But by that point, the rift had already begun.

John and Pastor Henry didn't converse much after that, although John did speak with plenty of people in the congregation. "Don't spread this around, but I think Pastor Henry is trying to drive me out of the church," John would intimate to his supporters. Because Pastor Henry was out of town often and because the church was so big, word didn't get back to the pastor until the damage was already done.

One Sunday, while giving announcements in the morning service, John announced his resignation—effective immediately in order to pursue "other interests." The next Sunday morning, John started another church, with a good number of people from his previous congregation.

What caused John to change, and how could a relationship that seemed so good turn into something so divisive? In the previous chapter, we examined Jezebel's manipulative influence within the church. If the Jezebel spirit symbolizes degenerative heart disease, the Lucifer spirit symbolizes a heart transplant—stealing the hearts of the people away from their leader. Just as the Jezebel spirit is predominant among women, so the Lucifer spirit is predominant among men.

John's transgression, and the genesis of the Lucifer spirit, can be traced back to the beginning of time—even before the fall of Adam and Eve in the garden. Let's examine the origin of sin and the beginnings of the Lucifer spirit.

LUCIFER: SON OF THE MORNING

How art thou fallen from heaven, O Lucifer, son of the morning! how art thou cut down to the ground, which didst weaken the nations! For thou hast said in thine heart, I will ascend into heaven, I will exalt my throne above the stars of God: I will sit also upon the mount of the congregation, in the sides of the north: I will ascend above the heights of the clouds: I will be like the Most High. Yet thou shalt be brought down to hell, to the sides of the pit.
—Isaiah 14:12–15

Although King Nebuchadnezzar of Babylon is implied to be Lucifer in the passage above, the implications go much further. We have already discussed previously that what is often singular and local in the Old Testament is corporate, boundless, and spiritual in the New Testament. With this in mind, in this passage King Nebuchadnezzar has been interpreted historically as a type of Satan.

Lucifer in Hebrew means, "shining one" or "morning star." In fact, *Lucifer* is the Latin term for the planet

Venus, which even to this day is referred to as the "morning star."

LUCIFER'S DOWNFALL

THE PROGENITOR OF THE FIRST CHURCH split was Lucifer. He convinced a great number of his underlings in heaven to join him, move across town, and start a new church. The Bible tells us that when he was thrown out of heaven, he took one-third of the angels with him (Rev. 12:3–4). Lucifer, who at one time served as one of heaven's principal angels, was expelled from heaven because he fell prey to the three *Ps—proximity, pride,* and *perceived injury.* If we can find out what went wrong with Lucifer, maybe it can help us too.

The Lucifer spirit is most pervasive among people involved in a support ministry: associate pastors, music ministers, cell group leaders, Sunday school teachers, elders, and the like. It is a divisive, splitting, rebellious spirit. Basically, it's strength lies in its utilization of illegitimate authority. As we already know, the use of illegitimate authority and rebellion is witchcraft.

Lucifer's primary means of motivation is false religion; what he offers is always a poor substitute for the truly spiritual. At times his counterfeits come across as bizarre and easy to detect, but at other times they may look as harmless as a stained-glass window. His perversions look valid enough to appear acceptable—by indulging in them surely no person would veer outside the parameters of "acceptable" Christian behavior.

Lucifer was perfect, he was wise, he was beautiful, he was liked, he was anointed, he covered the throne of God, and he was free to roam—to come and go as no other angel. There was no other angel who looked like him. Isaiah tells us that he was talented and beautiful. From all *appearances,* he had everything going for him.

So what happened to him? He was "heaven's associate pastor," right in the middle of everything, highly responsible, and in authority second only to the Trinity. He was the covering cherub, hovering over the Trinity from before the foundations of the earth. Just like John in our story, he was the associate every pastor dreamed of. Yet somewhere Lucifer took a wrong turn.

PROXIMITY: FAMILIARITY WITH GOD'S PRESENCE

LUCIFER WAS APPOINTED BY THE FATHER, Son, and Holy Spirit to minister *personally* to them in their Triune Presence. The other principle passage on Lucifer's beginnings, Ezekiel 28, tells us that at one time Lucifer was a guardian cherub: "Thou art the anointed cherub that covereth; and I have set thee so" (Ezek. 28:14). Cherubs operated as the primary guardians to the presence of God and hovered over the Trinity worshiping and serving them. No one was closer to the Godhead than Lucifer. *Proximity*—He entered and exited the presence of God at will. Perhaps he grew so accustomed to his privilege that he took the *right* to enter in for granted. People with this prerogative easily become too familiar with the presence of God. Even in his fallen state, Satan still enters the presence of God to accuse the believer before the Father. "For the accuser of our brethren is cast down, which accused them before our God day and night" (Rev. 12:10).

Talented and reliable cherub that he was, Lucifer was conferred with great authority. Because of his right to enter and exit the presence of God as he willed, he communicated with the angels as well as with the Trinity. Perhaps he started listening to some of the other angels. "Oh, Lucifer, you're so beautiful. You're such a talented musician; we've never heard any music like yours! Oh, Lucifer, you're so wise!"

For eons he gave all the glory to God. But at some point it shifted, and his heart changed. Instead of saying, "Lord, *You're* beautiful," he said, "You know, *I am* beautiful. *I am* stunning. *I am* quite wise." By virtue of his close proximity to God, he progressed to the second *P—Pride.*

PRIDE: WHO CREATED WHO?

LUCIFER BEGAN TAKING HIMSELF too seriously, and he forgot who created him. His close proximity to God opened his heart up to pride. This is common within the church leadership structure. Sometimes staff personnel, elders, home fellowship group leaders, and Sunday school teachers forget they are stewards and not owners of the ministry to which God has called them. When, after receiving a call and a vision from God, someone launches into a ministry, God will bring men and women to labor alongside the leader. But whose ministry is it?

We know everything belongs to God, but God always designates a leader—someone to be the head. The ministry does not belong to the person in charge, but God ordains one person to be the leader. Just as every family has a designated "head," so too, the pastor is the designated head of the local spiritual family.

Lucifer forgot who created him. People with a Lucifer spirit lose sight of the fact that they are stewards and suddenly think they are owners. "Why, the church wouldn't be anything without *me.* The reason God is blessing our church is because of *me.*" Even if it were true, wresting control of any kind from God's appointed leader is not justified. The one in charge may be perceived as slow, outdated, and behind the times, but his perceived shortcomings do not warrant an insolent response. The only warranted exception is a situation

36

where the leader has fallen into a grave sin such as per-version or heresy.

Any authority based in sedition or insurrection is rebellion. All rebellion is rooted in witchcraft—period. Influence of this kind is illegitimate and contrary to Scripture. People who fall into the trap of rebellion have forgotten that their calling is to support the one God called to lead.

The leader has given to the staff their jobs, salaries, visibility, and exposure. Sometimes the beneficiary of these privileges may develop a disease called the *"I wills."* Such an affected person begins to assert, *"I will* ascend above the mountain of God. *I will* be like the most High God"—just as Lucifer did in Isaiah 14. Suddenly he or she starts thinking that what belongs to someone else now belongs to him.

Ambition to serve or ambition to position?

An underlying motivation of a person who succumbs to a Lucifer spirit is selfish ambition. *Ambition* is defined as "the eager desire to achieve something." Ambition in itself isn't bad; in fact, it is a key character-istic of an effective leader. *Selfish* ambition, on the other hand, utilizes the arm of the flesh for the purposes of self-promotion, fame, or power. The word for *ambition* comes from the French word *ambile* which means "to go around for votes." A person with selfish ambition is driven to achieve status and influence for the purpose of self-promotion.

The Bible tells us that God promotes us. Promotion begins with servanthood. Jesus said, "Whoever desires to become great among you, let him be your servant" (Matt. 20:26, NKJV). A person intent on self-promotion had shown reason enough *not* to be promoted in lead-ership. The apostle Paul wrote in Philippians 2:3: "Do nothing out of selfish ambition or vain conceit, but in humility consider others better than yourselves" (NIV).

Ambition can easily transform itself into *selfish* ambition. This is the trap into which Lucifer fell. His ambition to *serve* turned into an ambition to *position.* So Lucifer started going around talking to other support staff—angels—saying, "You know, if *I* were God, I'd do things *differently* around here." They probably had a few prayer meetings, Bible studies, maybe even met over at Denny's for coffee. When they were around God, they appeared submitted, but as soon as church was over they plotted their strategy. Pay close attention to what happened next.

Perceived Injury

Ezekiel 28 gives us a glimpse into the background of Lucifer. It appears that Lucifer may have been an angel at the time God created the Garden of Eden.

> Thou hast been in Eden the garden of God. . . .
> Thou art the anointed cherub that covereth; and I
> have set thee so: thou wast upon the holy moun-
> tain of God; thou hast walked up and down in the
> midst of the stones of fire.
> —Ezekiel 28:13–14

At some point between creation of the earth and the deception of Adam and Eve in the garden, Lucifer was cast out of the presence of God. Perhaps Satan had ruled over the Garden prior to the creation of man and part of his reason for tempting Adam and Eve was his desire for his former position from which he had fallen.

This brings us to the last point. We began with *proximity,* then *pride,* and now we move to *perceived injury.* What originally began as heartfelt submission and praise to God ended in, "Well, I'm as good as He is. I don't need Them. I'll just do something on my own; all I need is a few hundred people." Could it be that Lucifer was still a guardian cherub when God was creating Adam and Eve? Now this is only conjecture, so be careful not to make a doctrine out of this, but because Lucifer covered the throne and, at one point as an angel, he was present in the Garden, I believe the probability is strong that he assisted God in His creative acts.

One day Lucifer realizes that man is going to be created in *God's* image, and he panics. "God has a new creation. I must not be good enough. After all I've done for God, He probably doesn't appreciate all the sacrifices I've made for Him. I'm probably going to be demoted. He's hiring another pastor. He doesn't appreciate my gift. I always *thought* that. Now I *know.*" Wait a minute; this isn't true at all! He's merely perceiving it. This information didn't come from the Father. It came from his imagination—*perceived injury.* How often do we perceive injury from others? Often, even before getting our facts straight, we begin dealing with perceptions—basing our feelings and reactions not on facts but on assumptions.

See how easily it can happen? People involve themselves in a church, then they take ownership of the ministry God has placed them in as stewards, and soon they become proud in their sphere of influence. But when things don't go the way they want them to, they're easily hurt. Out of their offense, the people pick up their marbles and go somewhere else where *they* can control their destiny. This occurs every day in congregations around the world. If it hasn't affected your church yet, it will. Sometimes persons with a Lucifer spirit will leave the church, taking other members with him. Others remain in the church and operate like a cancer from within.

The First Pentecostal Church was a thriving congregation. Although the church was growing, they were in dire need of leadership in their worship. Because so many people on the worship team wanted control, disagreements and bickering ran rampant. The lack of vision and the low level of excellence acted as hindrances to the ministry of the church.

When the church grew to the point that they were ready to bring a worship leader on staff, their pastoral search team located Steven, a talented young man with an unusual gift for leading people into the presence of God. Part of the interview process included a meeting with the worship team. Steve would be hired only upon the recommendation of the worship team members. Once the worship team arrived for the interview, Steve's chilly reception by certain members of the team turned the meeting into an awkward, solemn assembly. "How do you think the songs we sing on Sunday morning should be chosen?" Sam, one of the disgruntled members, asked.

"Well," Steve began, "I pray during the week, and then on Sunday we sing the songs I feel God leading us to sing. . . . "

"You know what's always worked for us," Sam interrupted, "we decide *together* what songs we sing. That's what the people in this church want."

Other members' smug comments and the general lack of response brought the interview to an abrupt close. After the unusually short meeting, the worship team discussed the subject of their interview. "I don't know why we have to hire a *professional* to lead worship," Sam complained. "How can an outsider understand the way our people respond? We don't need a worship leader; we're doing fine just as we are. Besides, there are better places to use the money that would be used for his salary." Three other people on the ten-member team concurred. Because the members couldn't reach an agreement about whether or not to hire Steve, they recommended not bringing him on staff. Shortly thereafter, four of the people who wanted to hire Steve resigned from the worship team. The desire for control among a few people stood in the way of what was best for the congregation.

As long as that spirit of Lucifer is allowed to flourish in that church, the team members with bad attitudes will act as a barrier to the Holy Spirit. Jesus said that a city divided against itself *cannot* stand (Matt. 12:25).

FAMILY DYNAMICS IN THE CHURCH

AT THE BEGINNING OF THE PREVIOUS CHAPTER I mentioned how the family is really a prototype of the local church. Whenever the roles of individual family members change, their family members jostle around until they find their new roles in the family. When a newborn baby enters the family, older siblings may be jealous of the attention given to the young infant. The parent certainly doesn't love them any less, but the older brother or sister may perceive that the parent doesn't love them as much. *Perceived injury.* The same is true in the church.

Whenever responsibilities change, the people affected by the change must jostle around to find and fit into a new role. The new position may not be as satisfying as the previous one. Perhaps the person's new role may entail more "behind the scenes" work rather than "up front" work. This is why servanthood is so important in the body of Christ. Leadership begins with servanthood. In fact, the function of leadership is to draw the congregation into doing what is best for *them,* not necessarily what is best for the leader. If it means the leader must work "behind the scenes," so be it.

The apostle Paul writes that the parts of the body not readily seen are the keys to the functioning of the whole body:

> Those members of the body, which seem to be more feeble, are necessary: And those members of the body, which we think to be less honourable, upon these we bestow more abundant honour; and our uncomely parts have more abundant comeliness.
>
> —1 Corinthians 12:22–23

Too quickly people assume that "visible" leadership positions are the most important. Is it easier to go through life without a hand or without a heart? A hand is one of the visible parts of the body that, although tremendously useful, we can live without. No one, however, can function without a heart. Which is more important, the visible or the invisible? In God's eyes, neither is more important than the other. Peter exhorts us in 1 Peter 5:6 to "humble yourselves therefore under the mighty hand of God, that he may exalt you in due time." Our purpose is to grow where we are planted and let God promote us.

When God blesses a church, and it begins to grow, change is inevitable. It cannot remain the same; new roles and relationships form, replacing the old roles and relationships. Anytime a new person is brought onto the team, other staff members may easily get jealous or fearful. They may be concerned about being replaced or of losing their position of influence. It may bother them that the new person is close to the pastor as they were before. Whenever there is pride in position, perceived injury is not far behind.

The natural reaction to perceived injury is to verbalize one's feelings to anybody willing to listen. At first

42

the offended person may be seeking comfort and solace, but a few ill-placed comments from the wrong people may plant seeds of malcontent. Nurtured over time, these seeds can grow into full-blown rebellion, witchcraft, and illegitimate authority.

Some people assume the church will fall apart if they are gone. "I'm the real reason for this church's success. Why, if I leave, all the people will leave with me." Try it and see. Some may go with you but not everyone. In all likelihood, half of the ones you take will go back, go somewhere else, or stop attending any church.

You may be a gifted associate pastor working on the staff of a large church. Perhaps you can preach better, have more words of knowledge, administrate better, or have more charisma than the pastor with whom you work. It's still not your vineyard. You have no right to split the body or take any part of it for yourself. If you undermine the authority of the person God has placed in leadership, you are operating in the spirit of Lucifer.

PROMOTION COMES FROM GOD

WHEN YOU BEGIN PROMOTING YOURSELF, your authority comes from *yourself,* not from *God.* By listening to the accolades of those who follow you rather than the voice of God, it's easy to get puffed up and start believing what the people say. Then when some disgruntled member suggests, "You ought to start a church because you're a better leader than Pastor So-and-So" you agree. Beware. Perceived injury is not far behind. If you do start your own church, God isn't the one who promoted you to lead it—you are! And you won't keep it. In fact, you will most likely lose it in the same way you stole it from someone else.

Follow only the person *God* has promoted and who has the full blessing of those in spiritual authority.

Promotion comes from the Lord, not from man. "For promotion cometh neither from the east, nor from the west, nor from the south. But God is the judge: he putteth down one, and setteth up another" (Ps. 75:6–7). If a man departs from a congregation with a cloud over his head to start another church, watch out. Lucifer may be lurking in the wings.

The story of the rise and fall of Absalom in 2 Samuel 13–20 is a prime example of someone with a Lucifer spirit. Because he was one of King David's sons, he had close proximity to the privilege and power that comes with the throne. His good looks and magnetic personality made him Israel's favorite son.

When his sister, Tamar, was raped and disgraced by their half-brother, Amnon, Absalom sought revenge. After seething for two years over the violation of his sister, Absalom seized the right opportunity and had his brother murdered. Having taken responsibility for committing a capital offense, he fled to the land of Geshur.

Now pay close attention. Nowhere in Scripture is there any indication that King David cast Absalom out of Israel. David mourned not only the death of Amnon, who had committed the rape, but also the fact that he was estranged from his other son: "But Absalom fled. . . . And *David* mourned for his son every day" (2 Sam. 13:37). Obviously, the initial estrangement from his father was only *perceived.* Absalom assumed his father was rejecting him.

Upon Absalom's return, King David found himself between a rock and a hard place. He welcomed the return of his son, but he also needed to keep his distance so that he wouldn't be accused of granting exclusive royal immunity to members of his own family. According to the laws of that time and according to the laws of Scripture, Absalom should have been put to death.

Eventually they were reconciled, but even then

Absalom took advantage of his royal privilege by usurping his father's influence over Israel. Remember that the root meaning of *ambition* is to "go around for votes." This is exactly what Absalom did. Every day he went to the city gate and conferred with the leaders, telling them what he would do differently than what his father the king was doing. Capitalizing on his father's shortcomings, he was able to garner enough votes to start an insurrection when the time was right. The end of Absalom was brutal and sudden as it often is with people who display a spirit of Lucifer (see 2 Sam. 18:9).

DEALING WITH LUCIFER AND JEZEBEL

IN THIS CHAPTER AND THE LAST, two of the more overt forms of witchcraft have been explained. Once they are identified, they must be dealt with redemptively. Below are a few keys to dealing with Lucifer and Jezebel:

Pray

Before deciding how to respond, it is imperative that you spend time in the presence of God. Prayer is the key. Without boldness, wisdom, and discernment, you are doomed to fall short. In Matthew 17:21, Jesus said there are certain spirits that "Goeth not out but by prayer and fasting." All too often, Spirit-filled believers rush in where angels fear to tread. We confront the person before the battle has been fought in the heavenlies, resulting in a messy situation that slowly draws the entire congregation into the fray. Bind and loose in the spiritual before binding and loosing in the natural (see Matt. 16:19).

Intercede on behalf of the person you believe to be influenced by a Jezebel or Lucifer spirit. Intercede for those in leadership. Above all, be sure that you are actually dealing with a demonic spirit. Throwing accusations of demonization without forethought—and fore-prayer—can do irreparable emotional damage to those in the body of Christ. Remember, the fallout in messy situations such as these can include people who were not even directly involved. Most of all, pray for wisdom in order to deal redemptively in the situation. The goal *is* restoration and reconciliation, *not* exclusion and removal.

JUDGE TO DELIVER, NOT TO KILL

WHAT IS YOUR INTENT AS YOU DELVE deeper into the problem? Do you have an ax to grind, or is it your heartfelt desire to redeem the person? The easy way out in situations such as this is to do anything possible to drive the problem person out of the church. Fortunately, God doesn't deal the same way with us! Are you judging to deliver or are you judging to kill? Perhaps as much as 90 percent of the church judge each other to kill.

If you were Pastor Henry in the example at the beginning of the chapter, how would you respond? Would you immediately deliver John over to Satan, or would you seek to restore him? It takes a bigger person to forgive and restore than it does to abandon or destroy. The heart of Jesus is the heart that restores.

GO IT ALONE

IT IS EASY TO OVERLOOK THE FACT that the binding and loosing mentioned in Matthew 18 applies first of all to discipline in the church. Jesus instructs us that when someone has trespassed against us, we should approach him or her individually with the hope of restoring the person (see Matt. 18:15–17). When approaching a person alone, sensitivity and discretion are the keys. Little progress is made if one of the parties becomes defensive.

Confronting someone when there are no witnesses can easily escalate into a case of the other person's word being pitted against yours. The temptation is to say too much at this level. If you do say too much, and your efforts are unsuccessful, you are certain to open a can of worms you may be unable to close.

A youth pastor was having difficulty with the behavior of one of the girls in his youth group. Her disruptions during the youth-group meetings seemed to become more pronounced when other members started participating in any discussions about the Bible. Growing tired of her antics, he called a meeting with the girl and her mother. Fortunately, he also brought the director of Christian education in on the discussion.

"The reason I called this meeting," the youth pastor began, "is to discuss your daughter. In our youth group meetings, she has become quite disruptive, and I want to talk about what can be done so this doesn't continue."

"The reason she is disruptive," the girl's mother shot back, "is because she says your youth group meetings are boring."

"Since the day I started working with the youth group at this church," the youth pastor continued, "your daughter has seemed determined to keep other youth from getting involved. Something needs to change." As the discussion progressed, the girl's mother became increasingly defensive of her daughter's actions. At one point the girl marched out of the room and slammed the door. Fifteen minutes later, her mother followed suit.

Determined to run the youth pastor out of the church, the girl's family started talking to other people in the congregation about what he had said in the meeting. "He doesn't like my daughter and said that he didn't want her in the youth group anymore," the girl's mother was heard saying. Fortunately, the Christian education director had been present. She was able to refute the family's accusations against the youth pastor. Had she not been present, the ensuing disagreement could have severely damaged the church and the ministry of the well-meaning youth pastor.

It may be advantageous to bring in a silent, independent, third party if the confrontation is potentially explosive. If you bring up an issue for the first time and you bring in a silent party, make sure that the discussion remains confidential and that your third party remains silent. If the third party is not perceived as independent, the person being confronted may view the confrontation as an opportunity for "ganging up."

BRING A FRIEND

SHOULD THE FIRST LEVEL PROVE TO BE UNSUCCESSFUL, repeat step one, but bring with you two or three "non-silent" witnesses. Draw upon church leaders who are spiritually mature and discerning. Remember to be sensitive as to how you articulate your feelings. Should your second attempt prove unsuccessful, move to the next step.

GO TO YOUR LEADER

IF YOU ARE IN LEADERSHIP, this is the time to act decisively. If there is no repentance, ease the person out of leadership. He or she may be your worship leader or an elder, but you are better off nipping the problem in the bud than waiting until it is a problem that could divide Christ's body. Remember that we live in a sue-happy society; thus, renouncing a person on a congregational level can be extremely risky.

Lucifer: Ambition to Position

When dealing with potentially explosive predicaments, it is imperative that you operate out of courage and not out of fear. As we studied in the previous chapter on Jezebel, no one had the courage to stand up to her. Ahab couldn't. Ahab's son, Ahaziah, wouldn't. Even Elijah struggled in his efforts to stand up to Jezebel.

Then Jehu came on the scene. This prophet, anointed by Elijah, refused to be intimidated by Jezebel. Jehu not only stood up to Jezebel but he also pursued her (see 2 Kings 9:30–37). In Jehu's perspective, Jezebel was flesh and blood just as he was. When we allow ourselves to become focused on what we see, we easily fall prey to intimidation.

DEALING WITH WITCHCRAFT IN YOUR OWN LIFE

AFTER READING THESE TWO CHAPTERS you may identify some characteristics in your life which resemble Jezebel or Lucifer. My advice to you is this: Deal with it quickly and decisively. The longer you wait to repent, the harder it is to leave the characteristics behind. Cut off any influences which might be planting seeds of witchcraft in your life. If you have offended someone, ask for their forgiveness, and make restitution if necessary. Last of all, submit yourself to the leadership God has placed in your church.

Lucifer was cast out of heaven. Jezebel was eaten by the dogs. Lucifer and Jezebel will spend eternity in the lake of fire. People who find their success at the expense of others will always find their just deserts . . . always.

In the next two chapters, we will examine Satan's covert operations in the church.

Five

SATAN'S GREATEST WEAPON

S UPPOSE FOR A MOMENT YOU were the devil. Ever since your disillusioning fall-out with God the Father, you were committed to the downfall of His kingdom. When Jesus appeared on the earth, you knew that your very existence was threatened. Should Jesus provide a once-for-all sacrifice for the sins of the people and win their hearts and minds, your defeat would be imminent.

At the end of Jesus' ministry, it appeared you had the upper hand. The Son of God was put to death on a cross, and it looked as if the divine plan of the ages were rendered powerless. But on the third day your plan for destruction was totally obliterated—Jesus rose from the grave, conquering death and hell. Making matters worse, the weapons of victory were now in the hands of your enemies—the very people you were intent on destroying. What would *you* do?

Although he knew he was defeated, Satan would not go down without a fight. He lost the war, but there were still battles that could be won. He changed his plan of attack: He would take as many people down with him as he could, and he would neutralize his enemies, blinding God's people to the defeat that he, the devil, had suffered. He would also do whatever he could to keep God's people from using their weapons.

To this day, Satan is still doing whatever he can to render the Christian powerless and impotent.

In this chapter, we will examine Satan's greatest weapon against the believer. Up to this point, we have looked at the devil's overt means of battling the church—manipulation, intimidation, and domination. Now, we will explore the more subtle aspects of witchcraft—legalism, guilt, and condemnation.

Legalism is so pervasive among many Christians that few even realize its extent. Further, the results of legalism—guilt and condemnation—reside in a place that is difficult to identify. But when the believer is released from legalism's grip, freedom and power abound.

The early believers wrestled with many of the same problems that the church faces today. Observe what the apostle Paul wrote to the church in Galatia:

> O foolish Galatians, who hath bewitched you, that ye should not obey the truth, before whose eyes Jesus Christ hath been evidently set forth, crucified among you? This only would I learn of you, Received ye the Spirit by the works of the law, or by the hearing of faith? Are ye so foolish? having begun in the Spirit, are ye now made perfect by the flesh? Have ye suffered so many things in vain?

if it be yet in vain. He therefore that ministereth to you the Spirit, and worketh miracles among you, doeth he it by the works of the law, or by the hearing of faith?

—Galatians 3:1–5

BEWITCHMENT AFFECTS BELIEVERS

WHAT MAKES THIS SCRIPTURE SO astonishing is the fact that the apostle Paul is writing about witchcraft's effect on born-again, Spirit-filled believers—people who had tasted, seen, and experienced the miraculous power of God. The believers in Galatia received the gift of the Holy Spirit and witnessed the working of miracles, and yet Paul says they were bewitched!

Did you know that a church can be filled with good, Spirit-filled people, and yet be oblivious to a move of God in their midst? They can hear an anointed word from the heart of God, but remain unable to respond—almost as if a spell had been cast on them. Many modern-day churches have one thing in common with the church in Galatia—bewitchment.

Bewitchment is "the power to mislead, using spells and hexes." The Greek word literally means "to smite or mislead with the eyes." Bewitchment—witchcraft—obscures what is in plain view.

Medieval fairytales are filled with stories about love potions which can cause a beautiful princess to fall in love with a not-so-handsome prince. The princess' perspective of the plain-looking prince was obscured. Today's newspaper and magazine ads extol the power of aphrodisiacs to cause two unlikely people to mysteriously fall in love. Aphrodisiacs and love potions are simply a means of bewitchment—they obscure what can be plainly seen.

WITCHCRAFT OBSCURES THE CROSS

JESUS HAD BEEN CRUCIFIED BEFORE the very eyes of some of the Galatian people, and yet they were unable to obey. Their bewitchment—witchcraft—obscured the cross.

If you were Satan, why would you want to obscure what happened at Calvary? Because the cross is where Jesus defeated Satan. Satan's only means of rendering his enemy—the church—powerless is to find some way to conceal or obscure the victory the believer has already won. It's the believers who pose a threat to Satan.

Satan expends a great amount of energy trying to keep people out of the kingdom of God. When a person gives his life to Jesus Christ, Satan changes his strategy. At this point Satan attempts to render the believer powerless and impotent. The last thing Satan needs is a believer who is intent on serving God and defeating the powers of hell. Herein is the dilemma: If Satan were to make a frontal assault on the believer, he could be identified and summarily defeated. However, if he could find a way to bewitch the believer with a tool of his own belief, he might have a chance to succeed. But in order to accomplish this, the power of the cross must be obscured.

GRACE OR WORKS

IF THE POWER OF THE CROSS LIES in what Jesus did for us apart from anything the believer could do to be good, then Satan would be able to obscure the cross by adding works back into the beliefs of the Christian. Grace operates in an "all or nothing" manner. Because it exists simply upon what cannot be earned, the moment works are added to the equation, grace is no longer grace. When believers lose sight of the cross, they inevitably go back to the works of the law.

Grace is received through faith—someone else accomplished it for us. Works can be identified in a million different ways.

CARNALITY: TRUSTING IN THE FLESH

ONCE BEWITCHED BY THE INFLUENCE of the enemy, the believer can go back under the law in two ways: carnality and legalism.

When I place my trust in any method or person apart from God, then I am using the arm of the flesh—carnality—and it brings me under a curse.

A church flourished under the guidance of a charismatic and dynamic pastor. When the pastor died, the church died with him. What happened? All things being equal, the people had placed their trust in the pastor and not in God. The pastor had relied on the charisma of his personality and his gifting rather than upon the power of the Holy Spirit to draw people in.

During a revival service a preacher challenged the audience to place their trust in God. He placed a challenge before them that if they wanted to serve God, they should come forward to the altar for prayer. He placed so much pressure upon the congregation to come forward, that nearly every person responded. Afterward the preacher praised God for the number of recommitments to Christ that night. What brought the people forward wasn't the Holy Spirit—it was the pressure the preacher placed on the audience! It was his insistence that if they did not come forward they would be seen by the rest of the congregation as people who needed to get right with God. The preacher used nothing more than an arm of his flesh—carnality—to force a response.

A ministry to feed the poor in Africa buys commercial time on a local television station, barraging the viewer with image after image of starving little children. Although the need is legitimate, the mission organization resorts to using guilt in order to raise the funds it so desperately needs.

Many believers try to argue non-Christians into the kingdom of God. No one has ever been argued into the kingdom of God. Only the Spirit of God can draw people in. But by relying on their debating abilities or their charisma, some leaders think they don't need the Holy Spirit's help.

When I trust in the arm of the flesh, what happens? My heart turns away from the Lord, and I trust everybody and everything but God. All the while I can be in the church, praising God, lifting my hands, saying hallelujah, and speaking in tongues—and still be cursed. What is the result of carnality? The cross of Jesus is obscured. We lose sight of what Jesus accomplished on the cross, and so we are unable to administer Jesus' victory.

LEGALISM: TRUSTING IN THE LAW

A VARIATION OF CARNALITY IS LEGALISM. Rather than trusting in the arm of the flesh, legalism places trust in rules and regulations. Legalism is one of the greatest stumbling blocks to new Christians, and it can be found in every congregation. It may be the greatest single problem we face as the western church.

In Paul's day, the debate in Galatia centered around the issue of circumcision. Certain Jewish Christians felt that the new Gentile believers should not only place their trust in Christ, but also take on the yoke of the Jewish law. As men gave their lives to Christ, the Galatian leaders insisted that they also be circumcised. Paul responded to the Galatians by reminding them that returning to the law brings the church under a curse from which she has already been redeemed: "For as many as are of the works of the law, are under the curse: for it is written, Cursed is every one that continueth not in all things which are written in the book of the law to do them" (Gal. 3:10). Because circumcision was part of the Mosaic law, the Galatian believers were going back under the curse.

The tendency among Christians throughout the ages has been to combine grace *and* works. Grace and works mix about as well as oil and water. Either we live by faith in the grace of Jesus Christ, or we live by the works of the law. Paul writes, "No man is justified by the law in the sight of God, it is evident: for, The just shall live by faith" (Gal. 3:11). There are two ways we can live—by the *law* or by *faith,* but we cannot live by both.

ALL OR NOTHING

WHEN THE BELIEVER RETURNS TO THE LAW, every jot and tittle must be adhered to. If the Galatian believers accepted circumcision but failed at any other point of the law, they were guilty of the entire law and no better than the unbeliever. Because every person is born with a sinful nature and cannot keep the law perfectly, he's condemned before he starts.

There is only one way to achieve righteousness with God—faith. It's a righteousness that comes through faith.

Righteousness simply means a person has been placed into a right relationship with God. When a person is made righteous, that person has the right to enter into a relationship with God, to commune with Him, to worship Him, and to spend eternity with Him.

Jesus abolished the law as a means of achieving righteousness. But He did not abolish the law; He fulfilled it. The law was faultless and perfect, revealing the nature, character, and holiness of God. But the law could no longer operate as a means of achieving righteousness with God. Jesus said, "Think not that I am come to destroy the law, or the prophets: I am not come to destroy, but to fulfil" (Matt. 5:17). The law stands forever, but we are not under the law, we're under grace. The Judaizers were coming to the born-again Jews, trying to pull them back under Sabbath-day laws—food laws, dietary laws: Do this, don't do that, wear this, don't wear that—putting them under all sorts of rules and regulations, bringing them back under the curse from which Jesus had redeemed them.

If we could be brought into a right relationship with God through the keeping of rules and regulations, then Jesus died needlessly. We wouldn't need Him.

LEGALISM IN THE CHURCH

MOST PEOPLE BELIEVE THEY HAVE TO KEEP a certain set of rules in order to stay right with God, but what makes you righteous does not depend on rules such as whether you don't smoke or don't drink. Please do not misunderstand, I am not advocating smoking and drinking. The simple point is this: There is only one way to be made right with God, and it's a righteousness that comes by trusting in what God accomplished through Christ at the cross. Drinking wine with your meal will neither make you righteous nor unrighteous. Abstaining from wine will neither make you righteous nor unrighteous. In Colossians 2:16, Paul says, "Let no man therefore judge you in meat, or in drink, or in respect of an holyday, or of the new moon, or of the sabbath days."

Many well-meaning churches impose legalistic practices upon their people. One denomination insists on meeting for worship on Saturdays only; another refuses to consider any day appropriate for worship but Sundays. Paul not only urged the Galatians to let no person judge them according to drink but also according to Sabbath days. If you want to keep the Sabbath, go ahead, but don't impose your convictions on your brother.

Churches with the strictest rules and regulations often have the greatest difficulty dealing with the sin it encounters in people. When a church responds to sin out of fear by imposing more law, that church simply opens itself up to more of the curse. The more sin they see, the more they impose the law. The more law they impose, the more rules there are to break. The more rules that are broken, the more law they impose. It becomes a vicious cycle that results in a defeated, life-less, impotent, mesmerized, bewitched church. The law will never make you right with God.

Will abstaining from meat on Fridays make you right-eous? Will wearing your hair in a bun, not wearing a wedding band, or wearing ten inches of extra dress length make you righteous before God? Not a bit. Only faith in Christ will usher in righteousness.

DENOMINATIONAL LAW

MOST CHURCHES THROW OUT THE LAW of Moses and replace it with a new set of laws. There's Baptist law, Pentecostal law, Word of Faith law, Assemblies of God law, Catholic law, Lutheran law, Wesleyan law—you name the denomination, each has its own set of laws. A church can even be "non-denominational," "interde-nominational," or "transdenominational" and have a set of laws which are as binding as the ordinances Jesus abolished at Calvary. A church may be steeped in reli-gious ceremonies and activities but be absolutely devoid of life!

Denominational rules, religious ceremonies, and church activities have a purpose in church life—they shape the life of a church, provide a foundation, a common ground from which to build the body—but they do not make one righteous. When they are used as a measure of righteousness, they have been used to obscure the cross and have become a bewitchment.

Legalism Looks Good and Religious

Legalism and trusting in the flesh are deceptive because they seem so good and look so religious. That is why both legalism and trust in the flesh are such a bewitchment. Every time I try to justify my actions or beliefs by keeping the rules, I step back into the flesh and move away from my faith-righteousness.

There is a group of churches that was founded by a man who at one time was a great healing evangelist. After he died, his followers picked up a teaching that denigrated the role of women. Even today, the women members of that sect aren't allowed to wear makeup and must keep their hair in a bun. In one assembly I'm familiar with, there are only about fifty people—most of whom are seventy years of age and older still clinging to that sect. They have no life, no regeneration, no one is getting saved, no joy, and worst of all, many are dying of terminal illness. Nobody gets healed. At one time, at least God used their leader to heal the sick. Their rigid rules are not healing or helping anyone get life.

What's wrong with these people? It isn't that they don't love God. They do love God. But they have placed themselves under the law. They try to earn God's love by what they wear, what they don't wear, how their hair is kept, and other legalistic rules. By departing from grace, one comes under the law. In

Romans 6:14, Paul says, "For sin shall not have dominion over you: for ye are not under the law but under grace." *When you go under the law, sin always has dominion over you!*

Legalism Leads to Guilt and Condemnation

Living under the oppression of legalism only brings bondage and slavery. Christians cannot operate in bondage and slavery for long before it begins to have adverse effects upon their lives.

Revelation 12:10 tells us that Satan is the accuser of the brethren, looking for any area he can find in our lives with which to accuse us as he stands before God day and night. When we live by the law and fall short, we give Satan all the weaponry he needs to shoot us down. The chief tools of the enemy—above any else— are guilt and condemnation.

Before leaving for work one morning, Jeff and Sherry had a sharp disagreement which ended when Jeff stomped out the front door. Their argument centered around what they would do later that evening. Jeff wanted to spend the evening at home. After driving all day in his car as an on-the-road salesman, the last thing he wanted to do in the evening was drive around more or be with people. Sherry, on the other hand, was home all day with their three kids. When her husband came home her greatest desire was to escape the family circus and converse with *real* people. Hence, their disagreement.

As Jeff drove to work, a subtle voice whispered in his ear, "Jeff, who do you think you are? You're not any good. What right do you have to be a leader at church? You're nothing but a hypocrite. You'll never be anything. You're a joke." Jeff was hearing good old-fashioned condemnation. If he accepted what the voice told him, he would feel guilty.

Condemnation is an accusation from the enemy which asserts: "You're no good. You'll never amount to anything." Guilt is what we feel if we accept and believe those statements: "You're right, I am no good, I'll never amount to anything." Every condemning voice comes from Satan. And most of the time it comes through the church.

Conviction is the result of the Holy Spirit's speaking into our lives. If the Holy Spirit had been allowed to enter Jeff's car, no doubt the Spirit would have spoken gently to Jeff: "You shouldn't have spoken to your wife like that. As soon as you get to the office, pick up the phone, call her, and apologize." Conviction can identify what's wrong, but conviction can also tell us what to do about the wrong in order to make things right again.

Suzanne was eight years old when she and her mother became born again. As she grew older, family pressures forced her to leave home and make a life for herself. Suzanne strayed away from God and soon discovered that she was pregnant. The baby's father didn't want anything to do with her or the baby and left her. Expecting to receive some help, she told her mother but instead received only rejection. Embarrassed by Suzanne's actions, her mother told her to keep away—especially from the church. Feeling rejected by her family and her boyfriend, she contemplated suicide. Suzanne finally decided to abort the child because she couldn't provide a home for it.

Suzanne felt isolated and confused. After the abortion, against her mother's advice, she contacted her pastor for counseling. He was very sympathetic. Suzanne recommitted her life to Jesus, and forgave her boyfriend, her family, and especially herself.

Suzanne returned to the church, but was met with derogatory comments from her former friends. When

Suzanne attempted to reconcile her relationship with her mother, she was rejected by her because she did not want to have the stigma of being a baby-killer's mother. Suzanne was crushed. The pain of rejection and the sting of guilt and condemnation drove Suzanne away from the church once again.

Hey, what happened here? Suzanne was convicted by the Holy Spirit, rededicated her life to God, and forgave everyone. She returned to the church hoping to receive forgiveness, but instead she was rejected with condemning words by her friends and family, and guilt drove her back out to the world.

The good news of Jesus Christ brings deliverance from condemnation and guilt, and shows people how Christ has already made righteous the believer who is in Christ. No one has been given the job of putting another person under condemnation. I can make a person feel guilty, and you can, too. It's second nature to most people. But when you do, you become a mouthpiece of the devil. Think about it; Satan's job is to accuse and condemn the brethren. So when you start flapping your jaws to condemn, you have yoked right up with Satan. You just became his TV or radio broadcaster or his personal ambassador, bringing condemnation to those around you. And one thing is as certain as death and taxes: You will reap more condemnation than you sowed!

It's much harder to convince people they've been made righteous than it is to show people they're not any good. It requires the power of the Holy Spirit and the Word of God to convince people they've been made righteous.

DEALING WITH GUILT AND CONDEMNATION

SATAN ACCUSES US before the Father day and night, but

the Word of God tells us that the righteous "overcame him by the blood of the Lamb, and by the word of their testimony; and they loved not their lives unto the death" (Rev. 12:11). To overcome the impact of the accusations of Satan, we must immerse ourselves in the blood of Christ, the precious Lamb of God. We must defeat the lies of Satan by the word of our testimony, willingly crucifying our lives and desires in order to rise to new life in Christ and to stand in His righteousness.

In Colossians 2:13–16, Paul states two ways whereby God made provision for us to be delivered from condemnation. First, he said all past sinful acts can be forgiven. Why? Jesus has already paid for them at the cross. Second, through the death of Jesus, God terminated the law of Moses as a means of achieving righteousness with God. If the law could still be used as a measure of righteousness, every time man wanted to come to God, Satan would be there to accuse a person of some broken statute, some broken code, or law. No one could keep the law perfectly. It became a barrier that hindered all from getting to God. So through the death of Jesus, God nailed that law, that barrier, to the cross. Not even Moses, the lawgiver, was able to measure up to the law. When he lost his temper, he forfeited his inheritance of entering the Promised Land.

Paul writes in Romans 6:6: "Knowing this, that our old man is crucified with him, that the body of sin might be destroyed, that henceforth we should not serve sin." When Jesus died on the cross, our old man—that rebellious carnal nature—was crucified with Christ. But although Jesus nailed our rebellious nature to the cross, His sacrifice at Calvary will do no good unless we know about that sacrifice and respond properly to His grace. Later in the same chapter, Paul counsels the believer: "Likewise reckon ye also yourselves to be dead indeed unto sin, but alive unto God through Jesus Christ our

Lord" (Rom. 6:11). In other words, what Christ accomplished for us on the cross is an accomplished act in the past. But we have to recognize it and acknowledge it by faith for it to do us any good.

The good news for every believer is this: The execution of your old man—your rebellious nature—took place two thousand years ago. The problem is, you still want to help God out by doing something to right our wrongs. Your old man has one destiny in God, and it's called *execution*. The only thing good you can do about the old man is to make sure he's dead. You can't reform him, you can't give him religion, you can't pray him through, you can't change his character. The only thing you can do to the old man is kill him. God's remedy is the execution of your old man. Isn't that lovely? God's desire is for the *new* man, *Christ,* to be formed in you.

Romans 8:1 tells us, "There is therefore now no condemnation to them which are in Christ Jesus." As long as I'm living under condemnation, I am no threat to Satan. That's why he wants to keep me there. The only people who can effectively deal with Satan are those who have escaped condemnation through the cross. Jesus died to rescue you from bondage, but as long as you're under condemnation of any kind, you can never live in the freedom of Romans 8.

For centuries, the church has operated like this: living in the defeat of the old man. Paul says there is now therefore no condemnation to those who are—here's the only condition—*in Christ Jesus*. If you are *in* Christ your sins are covered by His blood. If you're *out* of Christ you're living under condemnation. You've been sentenced to die. You're just like a prison inmate, sitting on death row. Oh, you eat, you drink, you watch TV, you live out your life on earth, but you are waiting for the sentence of death. Everyone who believes on Jesus is *in* Christ, where *no* condemnation exists.

ADMINISTERING THE VICTORY

ON THE CROSS JESUS administered a total, irreversible, and eternal defeat to Satan. Nothing in this age or any age to come can ever change the victory Jesus won over Satan.

In the second section we're going to discover the scriptural basis for walking in the fullness of our freedom in Christ. Using this knowledge, you will then discover how to use it in the context of spiritual warfare. In the third section, we will look at the power of the cross in the life of the believer.

Part II

DEFEATING SATAN AND THE POWER OF WITCHCRAFT IN YOUR LIFE

Six

FIVE KEY PRINCIPLES OF THE KINGDOM

HAVE YOU EVER WONDERED WHY the lives of many Christians seem no different than the lives of non-Christians? If Jesus defeated witchcraft and the powers of hell two thousand years ago at the cross, why aren't there more believers living in victory? Although Jesus did win the victory, many Spirit-filled Christians fail to apply the power of the cross to their lives. We forget what Jesus accomplished for us on the cross and listen to the lies of the enemy: "You're worthless! You'll never amount to anything"—and we believe him. But to fight the enemy effectively, we must understand the magnitude of Jesus' sacrifice in order to rescue us from the bondage of witchcraft, death, and sin.

In this chapter, we are going to examine how Jesus

uses the cross to move us *beyond* the point of salvation. As we free ourselves from the control of witchcraft, there are five, key life-changing principles of the kingdom of God that give the basis for our release from the powers of hell.

1: THE CROSS IS THE ONLY BASIS FOR THE PROVISION OF MY NEEDS

PEOPLE LIVING UNDER THE INFLUENCE of witchcraft assume that God blesses them according to their good works. They convince themselves that "God helps those who help themselves"—as if our good deeds could ever amount to anything. Isaiah 64:6 says "we are all as an unclean thing, and all our righteousnesses are as filthy rags." When our good works fall short, we fall under guilt and condemnation and see no reason why God would ever want to help us. Fortunately, God doesn't supply our needs according to our good works but "according to his riches in glory by Christ Jesus" (Phil. 4:19).

It's good news that God isn't limited to helping only those who help themselves—or none of us would ever receive anything from God. The only door through which you can approach God for the supply of your needs is the door of the shed blood of Christ upon the cross. There is no other way to have your needs met, whether they are physical, spiritual, or eternal. You can never be good enough to merit God's favor, so you might as well trust in the grace of God—the evidence of God's unmerited favor upon your life.

Without the cross we have no access to God, no righteousness, no fellowship, and no inheritance in Him. Hebrews 10:14 says, "For by one offering [the sacrifice of Jesus Christ] he hath perfected for ever them that are sanctified." In other words, on the basis of the eternal sacrifice of Jesus Christ, you, I—every believer—are in the continual process of being cleansed, purified, and made right with God.

God didn't start out with fifty-two plans. Since the beginning He has had just one plan—the death of Jesus, the Lamb slain from the foundation of the world. Jesus wanted to be the curse, He wanted to be my rejection, taking away my sin and rebellion, so I could have acceptance with the Father. It was God's plan from ages past that by one sacrifice we could all be made right with God. Hebrews 10:12 tells us that after Jesus offered the one sacrifice for sin, He sat down at the right hand of God. Why did Jesus sit down? Because He would never have to do it again. One sacrifice forever in Christ Jesus.

It was in the cross that God planned the meeting of all our needs, large and small. The cross is the sole basis of all God's provisions for the sons of Adam. Forgiveness, healing, release from shame, sorrow, and poverty are all accounted for in the cross.

#2: AT THE CROSS JESUS ADMINISTERED A TOTAL, PERMANENT, IRREVERSIBLE DEFEAT UPON SATAN

SATAN HAS ALREADY BEEN DEFEATED. When our sins were nailed to the cross, Jesus made a public spectacle of Satan, triumphing over him and removing his weapons forever (Col. 2:15). Satan's weapons for fighting the righteous are gone. It's as if the roaring lion who seeks whom he may devour just had his teeth removed. We still need to be vigilant, but the battle has already been won! It isn't something that's *going* to happen. Satan has *already been defeated*. It's an accomplished fact!

It isn't our responsibility to defeat Satan. We couldn't defeat Satan by ourselves if our lives depended on it. But it is our responsibility to apply the victory that Jesus

71

already won at the cross. And we apply that victory to our own lives as we appropriate Christ's victory and enter into His presence and power. We appropriate His victory by using our faith and taking His victory as ours.

It's just like the child who spends his daddy's money. Because he is an heir, he lives in his daddy's house and enjoys the privileges that go along with being an heir. The son didn't earn the inheritance and he didn't do anything to deserve it; he just happened to be his daddy's son. So it is for the believer. I must appropriate what Christ earned for me. I didn't win the victory, Jesus did. I apply that victory as mine because I am an heir with Christ.

#3: GOD WANTS TO TRANSPORT YOU FROM THE KINGDOM OF DARKNESS INTO THE KINGDOM OF LIGHT

GOD DELIVERED MANKIND FROM the authority of the wicked one and placed him under the authority of the Lord Jesus.

> Giving thanks unto the Father, which hath made us meet to be partakers of the inheritance of the saints in light: Who hath delivered us from the power of darkness, and hath translated us into the kingdom of his dear Son: In whom we have redemption through his blood, even the forgiveness of sins.
> —Colossians 1:12–14

Notice the verse says that through redemption we have been delivered from the power of Satan—the kingdom of darkness—and carried over into the kingdom of the light of God's dear Son.

The word for *power* used here is *exousia,* the same word that is used for *authority* (see 1 Cor. 15:24). We have been delivered out of the authority of Satan's kingdom and placed under a new authority, a new rule, a new kingdom, called the kingdom of God.

It's important to notice that Satan does have authority. It may be limited, but he does have authority. How can one be translated out of the authority of Satan into the authority of God if Satan had no authority?

Where does Satan get his authority? He gets it from every person who is in rebellion against God. Satan is the great chief rebel and liar; anybody who is in rebellion against God is automatically under the authority of Satan. Paul is speaking to the believers when he says, "And you hath he quickened, who were dead in trespasses and sins; Wherein in time past ye walked according to the course of this world, according to the prince of the power of the air, the spirit that now worketh in the children of disobedience" (Eph. 2:1–2).

There are two Greek words for *air;* one speaks of the domain surrounding heaven (*ouranos*) and one speaks of the domain over the earth (*aer*). The second idea pertains in this passage. Satan is the ruler in the realm of authority over the atmospheric area above the earth. *Vine's Expository Dictionary* defines *air* this way: "the sphere in which the inhabitants of the world live and which, through the rebellious and godless condition of humanity, constitutes the seat of his [Satan's] authority." That is why Satan is called the prince of the power of the air.

By what authority does Satan, a defeated foe, have the right to influence the people of the earth? Because as children of disobedience, they inhabit Satan's seat of authority—his sphere. You can only be in one kingdom at a time. If you are obeying God and are obedient to His Son, Jesus Christ, you have a right to be in God's kingdom. But if you have rejected the Lord Jesus Christ, you are in Satan's kingdom. Why? Because you are a son of disobedience, just like Satan.

Satan may be a usurper of God's authority, but he has legitimate authority over every person who is in rebellion against God. Satan, the chief rebel, rules over *all* other rebels. You may have been transferred into the kingdom of God, but if you allow the spirit of rebellion to rule in your heart, God is not ruling over you, Satan is. He then is able to exercise his influence not only over those who were never saved, but also over many Christians who have given themselves over to rebellion. Rebellion places them under the influence of a kingdom from which God had previously delivered them.

That's why rebellion is called witchcraft. People are mesmerized into believing that since they are in God's kingdom, they are immune to the influence of Satan. But rebellion links us with Satan, so it links us with a curse and to the kingdom of darkness. That is why a person with a Lucifer or a Jezebel spirit can be a Christian and yet operate as an implement of destruction within the church. A person can be bought, paid for, sealed, and delivered to heaven, and yet be used as a tool of the enemy on earth.

Because we are all linked to Adam through natural birth, we are all born with a sinful, rebellious nature: "Among whom also we all had our conversation in times past in the lusts of our flesh, fulfilling the desires of the flesh and of the mind; and were by nature the children of wrath, even as others" (Eph. 2:3). *No parent has ever had to train a child to disobey*—every person born is a perfect copy of Adam. We are all members of "the Adams family." From the moment of birth disobedience reigns. David wrote, "I was shapen in iniquity; and in sin did my mother conceive me" (Ps. 51:5). David did not mean that the sexual act was a sin, but that his sin nature developed right in the womb of his mother.

In every descendant of Adam there is the nature of a rebel. Adam's children were born after the Fall, and so every human being that has descended from Adam has the nature of a rebel. It came with birth. And that nature makes one subject to the authority of Satan.

Thank God we have good news; there is a way out of Satan's kingdom, a way out of darkness into the light of God's dear Son.

#4: Our Bridge Out of Darkness Is Jesus Christ

IMAGINE A GREAT RIVER. On one side is the kingdom of God and light. On the other side of the river lies the kingdom of darkness and the domain of Satan. What do you do if you want to leave the kingdom of darkness and pass over to the kingdom of light? You may be tempted to swim on your own, but the river is too deep, too fast, and too wide. What you need is a bridge, which God provides. There's only one, and that bridge is Jesus Christ and His shed blood.

#5: The Bridge Is the Gateway to the Destination

A BRIDGE IS NOT AN END—but a means to the destination. Jesus is the Bridge to the kingdom of light. Colossians 1:13 says Christ "hath delivered us from the power of darkness, and hath *translated* us into the kingdom of his dear Son" (italics added). Jesus Christ is the bridge, but His goal is to get us into the *fullness* of His kingdom. He wants to take us out of one kingdom and place us into another. The problem is, millions of believers have been transferred out of the kingdom of darkness via the Bridge of Christ Jesus, but they never crossed to the other side. Thank God they're out of the kingdom of darkness, but salvation isn't the end; it is just the beginning. It's a way into the kingdom of God.

I'm not minimizing the importance of salvation, but God has so much more for His church than just salvation. God's desire is for us to rule with Jesus Christ in this life as kings and priests. He said in Revelation 5:10 that God has made us kings and priests with the purpose of reigning with Christ *now,* not in some ethereal millennium way out yonder.

Paul writes in Romans 5:17, "For if by one man's offence [speaking of Adam's sin] death reigned by one; much more they which receive abundance of grace and of the gift of righteousness [notice righteousness is a gift] shall reign in life by one, Jesus Christ." Now where are you? Are you hanging around the bridge? Or are you reigning in life with Jesus? Are you experiencing everything God has for you? Few people realize that God is just as concerned about this life as He is about the next. Through Christ, the Perfect Man—or, in keeping with 1 Corinthians, chapter 15, "the Second Man"—the last Adam, I can reign with Jesus in this life. Right now. I challenge you to go beyond salvation— walk across the bridge and enter the full purposes of God for this generation.

Seven

LAST ADAM FIRST

IMAGINE A BATTLEFIELD WHERE TWO ENEMIES are preparing to confront one another. Both sides have spent hours strategizing, organizing into battalions, and stockpiling their weapons. Just as the battle begins, one side realizes something is missing—they forgot to bring their bullets! They have their guns, but they don't have the ammunition to make their guns effective. It doesn't take a genius to figure out which side will win the battle.

Before the believer's spiritual weapons are explained in the next chapter, I want to give you some ammunition. Many Christians go into battle with their weapons, but they have no ammunition. Without bullets, a gun is useless. In this chapter you will find anointed "bullets" to use for the times when Satan tells you that you will never change, that your spouse will never change, that your children will never change.

In this chapter, you will see how Jesus went back to the beginning of mankind to eradicate our sin. A person pulling dandelions from his front yard doesn't merely remove what is in plain view. To ensure that they don't grow back, dandelions must be pulled out *roots and all*. We learned in chapter one that the root is the key to the fruit. When dealing with sin, you have to get to the root in order to get rid of it. In this chapter, we are going to get to the root of sin.

SATAN'S PLAN FOR MAN'S SIN

AN IMPORTANT PRINCIPLE FOR SHARING the gospel with unbelievers is to communicate that God loves them and has a wonderful plan for their life. Did you know that Satan has a plan for your life as well? Satan's plan is to breed sin into the human race as a means to overcome his enemy and past employer, God. When Satan deceived Adam, sin entered into the descendants of Adam, the Adamic race. Paul says that Adam was a pattern of things to come (Rom. 5:14). Since Adam, all humanity has resident within them the pattern of sin.

Before their sin, Adam and Eve were naked, clothed only in the glory of God, and together the three walked in intimate communion. After their sin, when God came around to walk with them, Adam and Eve hid themselves because of their guilt, shame, and condemnation (Gen. 3:8). Do you see the weapons Satan has been using since the very beginning? It's so devious. Satan lures us into sin and then condemns us for doing what he tried to get us to do in the first place! Then he deceives us into thinking that we can correct our transgressions by being good. That's where legalism and the law enters in. Can you see the vicious cycle? It began in the garden, and it's still going strong today.

But God had another plan wrapped in another Adam, named Jesus. When Jesus came, He became the last Adam, the final representative of the Adamic race, taking upon Himself all of the guilt, sin, curse, and condemnation of Adam's transgression.

TWO ADAMS

WHEN GOD LOOKS AT THE HUMAN RACE, He sees two men—the first Adam, and the last Adam. The Bible says you're either in one or you're in the other. "In Adam all die," Paul writes in 1 Corinthians 15:22, "[but] even so in Christ shall all be made alive."

When Jesus rose from the dead there were only two representatives of the human race—the first Adam and the last Adam. "For as by one man's disobedience [the first Adam] many were made sinners, so by the obedience of one [Jesus] shall many be made righteous" (Rom. 5:19). You inherited the seed of sin because you are a physical descendant of Adam. You had no choice whether to accept or reject this seed of sin, just as you had no choice whether or not to be born.

When Jesus went to the cross, He took upon Himself Adam's sin and the curse, and died as the last Adam. Three days later He rose again as the progenitor of a brand-new race that had never existed before.

By the obedience of one—Jesus Christ—we were given the opportunity to receive the gift of righteousness. Our relationship to Adam was involuntary; but our relationship to Jesus Christ is voluntary. When you accept Jesus by faith, God no longer counts the sins of your past against you. Praise God, our forgiveness is retroactive! That's our release from the influence of witchcraft. No judgment, no damnation, no death sentence can ever come upon us.

A WARRANT FOR YOUR DEATH

SIN HAS A PENALTY—DEATH. "For the wages of sin is death" (Rom. 6:23). The day you were born, you were issued a death warrant. Because all people are born in sin, and sin's penalty is death, there must be a death—a sacrifice—on behalf of each person. Without a death, sin can never be forgiven.

From Moses until Jesus, the Jews relied upon the death and blood of animals as an atonement for their sin. *Atonement,* according to *Vine's Expository Dictionary,* is "the means (in and through the Person and work of the Lord Jesus Christ, in His death on the cross by the shedding of His blood in His vicarious sacrifice for sin) by which God shows mercy to sinners." God made an *atonement*—a sacrifice—for our guilt and sin in Adam's race through the blood of Jesus. Everyone who trusts in Jesus—the last Adam—for their salvation has the guilt of the first Adam removed. Through Jesus Christ, we can be brought into a right relationship with God without guilt or condemnation.

By the blood of Jesus, God forgives all of our past acts of disobedience. Paul says that in Christ, God "forgave us *all* our sins" (Col. 2:13, NIV, italics added). How many of our sins does God forgive? *All* of them. If God can't forgive all sin, then the blood of Jesus was not powerful enough to overcome Satan. Even if one sin was left unforgiven, we could never have access to God. So He forgives all of them. God has made it possible for us to be assured that all of our sinful acts have been forgiven.

DEATH RELEASES US FROM OUR INDEBTEDNESS

LET'S FINISH PAUL'S THOUGHT in Colossians 2:13–14:

> When you were dead in your sins and in the uncir-
> cumcision of your sinful nature, God made you
> alive with Christ. He forgave us all our sins, having
> canceled the written code, with its regulations,
> that was against us and that stood opposed to us;
> he took it away, nailing it to the cross (NIV).

What was the written code that Jesus nailed to the
cross? It's the law. The Greek word in this passage literally refers to a certificate of indebtedness. People who
live by the law find themselves increasingly in debt to
sin. No matter how hard they try to pay it off, it seems
as if the debt grows greater and greater. The better they
try to behave, the more in bondage to sin they become.

One of the anointed bullets available to us is a recog-
nition of the fact that death releases people from their
indebtedness. Once a person is laid in the grave, debts
no longer remain outstanding. How can you collect
from a person who is deceased? When a person cannot
pay off a debt he owes to the Mafia, he may be released
from his obligation—but it will cost him his life. Jesus
took our certificate of indebtedness—the law—and by
His death on the cross, paid it, setting it aside as a
means of achieving righteousness with God.

When our certificate of indebtedness was nailed to
the cross, the need for the law came to an end: "For
Christ is the end of the law for righteousness to every
one that believeth" (Rom. 10:4).

The first Adam brought the need for successive generations of the human race to fulfill the requirements of
the law; the last Adam, Christ, brought an end to the
law. Christ is the end of the law as a means of achieving
favor and righteousness with God. Hallelujah! The
length of your hair, the makeup you decline to wear,
whether or not you say a bad word, none of that will
make you righteous. Our righteousness comes only

through the shed blood of Jesus Christ.

OUR RESPONSE TO WITCHCRAFT

WITCHCRAFT TRIES TO OBSCURE what the last Adam accomplished for us on the cross. Satan comes to us and tells us, "You've gotta help God out a little. You didn't do enough. You didn't do right. You didn't say enough. You had this wrong thought; that wrong attitude." When we entertain those thoughts, we walk in condemnation, and we're then unable to walk by faith. But if we walk in the full knowledge of what Christ accomplished at Calvary, then the enemy won't have room to condemn us anymore. When we hear those voices saying, "You aren't doing enough," we can respond with, "I'm not walking in my righteousness; I am walking in His righteousness, and He is the end of the law to all that believe." Such a response is a second bullet available to defeat the enemy's attack.

Before Christ, God used the law in order to provide a temporary means of righteousness. Today, we don't need the *law* in order to achieve righteousness with God. Through *faith* we now obtain righteousness with God.

ABRAHAM: THE MODEL OF FAITH—RIGHTEOUSNESS

EVEN BEFORE MOSES GAVE THE LAW to Israel, God raised up a model of faith righteousness. Abraham stands as another bullet—the ammunition we use in our own walk in faith righteousness. About half a millennium before Moses, when Abraham and Sarah were past their child-bearing years, God gave a promise to Abraham that He would make his descendants as numerous as the stars in the sky. Abraham believed God, and it was credited to him as righteousness. It's right there in

Genesis 15:6. The key to Abraham's righteousness was not in the law, it was in his belief in God.

Abraham believed the promise that not only would his children be as numerous as the stars in the sky but that through him, the whole world would be blessed. Two thousand years later the world was blessed by Abraham's seed—Jesus Christ. Abraham lived before the law, but was saved through faith, just as we are. Abraham expressed his faith looking forward. From this side of the cross, we express our faith, looking back to the event when Jesus came, shed His blood, and died on Calvary.

People may look at Abraham as a great man of faith and believe that he was an exceptional example. But don't forget that Abraham failed many times. Twenty-three years after God promised to make Abraham's descendants as numerous as the stars in the sky (Gen. 15:5), Abraham and Sarah grew impatient and took God's promise into their own hands (Gen. 16). Sarah gave her maid to Abraham to bear children on Sarah's behalf. Nine months later, Hagar gave birth to Ishmael.

Was that God's will? What right did Hagar have to be included in God's promise to Abraham? She wasn't even Abraham's covenantal wife. Some people say Abraham staggered not—I'd say Ishmael's a pretty big stagger. Since the birth of Isaac to this very day, the descendants of Ishmael and Isaac have been at odds.

In Genesis 20, Abraham gave his wife to a heathen king. Because Sarah was beautiful, he was afraid someone would kill him in order to take her away. Abraham concocted a story and told everyone that she was his sister. Believing she wasn't married, the king took her into his harem. Abraham and Sarah responded by saying and doing nothing. If it hadn't been for God's intervention, Abraham would have lost his wife and maybe even his life. He nearly counteracted God's promise.

It was Abraham's faith that made him righteous to God, though he failed many times. Even if I fail in some area of my life, my faith is still being reckoned to me as righteousness. Praise God! That doesn't mean I go out and do whatever I want. Nor do I try to earn my righteousness by keeping a set of laws. Our righteousness comes through faith in the last Adam, Jesus Christ.

JESUS UNDID WHAT ADAM HAD DONE

JESUS, THE LAST ADAM, and our greatest ammunition against Satan, undid what the first Adam had done. In His death, Jesus took your place, once for all, from the first Adam forward through today. He stood in your place as your substitute to take God's judgment and wrath so you could encounter God's love, acceptance, and forgiveness.

When you come to Jesus for salvation, trusting in Him to remove your sin, your faith is credited to you as righteousness. God looks at you as though you are already in a right relationship with Him. The same could be true of anyone who was able to obey the law completely—but unfortunately, only one person is able to obey every law. The one person able to keep the law is the one who fulfilled it—Jesus. When we give our lives to Him, the righteousness of Christ covers us, and God sees us as though we have kept the law completely. On my own, I can't keep the law. Neither can you. But God sees us as perfect through the blood of Jesus.

When Satan says to you, "You're mired in sin. You've always been a Jezebel, and you always will be a Jezebel." You can come back at him with, "Satan, you're mired in your own sin. You've always been a liar, and you always will be a liar. I was mired in sin, but through the blood of Jesus, the last Adam, the penalty of sin is reversed, and now I have life in Jesus Christ!"

When we arm ourselves with anointed bullets, and we walk in the knowledge of what Christ accomplished for us on the cross, we can withstand the wiles of the enemy and enjoy the kind of life God destined for every person.

Eight

THE NATURE OF SPIRITUAL WARFARE

DID YOU KNOW THAT IF YOU are a Christian, you're in a state of war? When you give your life to Jesus Christ, you join a war "already in progress." You might say, "Well, I don't have a gripe with anybody. I don't mess with the devil, and he doesn't mess with me."

Let's say you are a citizen of the United States, and the president and ruling authorities declare war on Russia. It doesn't matter whether or not you're a pacifist, if you are a citizen of the United States, you're at war because your government has declared war. As a citizen in the kingdom of God, you are at war with the devil. Your spiritual position is that of a citizen in God's kingdom, but your spiritual function is to serve as a soldier in the battle between light and darkness.

Did you know that as a soldier in God's army you could be asked to lay down your life? Maybe you thought you were just a witness. The Greek word for *witness* comes from the same word as *martyr.* A *witness*—a *martyr*—is someone willing to lay his life down for what he believes. But before a Christian dies for what he believes, he must first be willing to die to himself—to self, to the law, to ambition, to career. A good soldier subordinates his or her needs for the sake of a higher authority.

WE EXERCISE JESUS' AUTHORITY

ALTHOUGH JESUS TRIUMPHED OVER SATAN, He expects God's people to enforce the victory. After Jesus rose from the grave He had this to say to His disciples:

> All authority in heaven and on earth has been given to me. Therefore go and make disciples of all nations, baptizing them in the name of the Father and of the Son and of the Holy Spirit, and teaching them to obey everything I have commanded you. And surely I will be with you always, to the very end of the age.
> —Matthew 28:18–20, NIV

When Jesus defeated the powers of death and hell, He gained, once for all, the authority over Satan. Notice He says, "*All* authority in heaven and on earth has been given to Me." Jesus has all authority. His next sentence is then prefaced with a "therefore." Why is it there? *Therefore* can also be interpreted as "hence" or "with this in mind." Jesus was saying to His disciples that He has all authority; with this in mind, make disciples. Jesus' authority has a bearing on the way we make disciples. It's our decision whether or not to exercise the authority Jesus obtained over Satan. Jesus' authority doesn't do us any good unless we appropriate it.

You have a choice when "the enemy's delivery service" suddenly turns up on your doorstep with a package that you did not order. The delivery service insists that the seasonal gift—a parcel containing the flu—has been delivered to every home in the neighborhood, and now you have the privilege of receiving it. Knowing that Jesus died for your sicknesses and disease, in His name you can slam the door in the enemy's face—but you can also choose to do nothing and effectively receive it.

The authority we assert over the enemy depends upon the victory Jesus won over Satan. No Christian defeats the devil on his or her own. We merely appropriate and administer the victory Jesus won. Even if we pray for a person and a demon comes out, it's not me, it's Jesus in me. "Christ in you, the hope of glory" (Col. 1:27). We're merely enforcing the victory over the power of the enemy.

I used to be a shy, timid Baptist who didn't know how to walk in the victory Jesus won. I had all the legal rights over the enemy, but I never administered them. All the legal rights to pray for the sick, to cast out demons, to see people saved, and to rebuke the adversary, but I failed to administer them. I just sat and hoped that by osmosis the enemy wouldn't get me. But victory has to be enforced, or it's no authority.

It's like the couple on their way home from church. As the husband and wife drive up to their home, they discover a U-haul van parked in their driveway. A man, obviously a burglar, is moving the furniture from their house into the van. Still in the car, the wife turns to her husband and says, "He doesn't have a right to do that. We own that furniture. It doesn't belong to him. That's illegal."

The husband then replies, "You're absolutely right, honey. He can't do it. Let's go get a bite to eat."

ASSERTING AUTHORITY REQUIRES AGGRESSION

WHEN THE COUPLE RETURNS TO THEIR HOME, all their furniture is gone. Why? They had the legal right to stop the burglar, but they didn't enforce it. They didn't even call the police to enforce their rights. There are countless Christians who stand by and watch as the devil steals from them. They have no idea how to stop the pillaging. The key to walking in the authority of Jesus is to enforce His authority. If you don't, Satan will steal, kill, and destroy.

Enforcing the authority of Jesus requires aggression. The kingdom of God suffers violence, and the Bible says *who* takes it by force? Not the timid, but the violent:

> And from the days of John the Baptist until now the kingdom of heaven suffereth violence, and the violent take it by force.
>
> —Matthew 11:12

In spiritual warfare you have to be aggressive—aggressive in praise, aggressive in prayer, aggressive in proclaiming the Word of God. Without an aggressive counterattack, the devil ain't gonna get you nothing but killed in the kingdom of God. I promise you that.

TWO EXTREMES

CHRISTIANS GENERALLY GO TO ONE OF TWO EXTREMES. First, they think the continual battles they engage in with the enemy will determine the ultimate victory. People who assume this become transfixed with the idea of spiritual warfare. Because everything is a battle, they see a demon under every rock. Colossians 2:15 tells us that Jesus not only disarmed the rulers and authorities, but "he made a public spectacle of them, triumphing over them" (NIV). Jesus made a public spectacle so that everyone could see that the war is over—the victory is won.

The other faulty assumption people make is thinking that because the devil is defeated, there's nothing left to do. People who live by this rule are fatalistic, assuming that anything that happens to them must be God's will. The irony of this mindset is they are content with whatever life gives them. Often, by doing nothing, they live in defeat and experience so much less than God's best. Satan has been defeated, *but he hasn't been taken into captivity!*

During the Gulf War, Iraq was soundly defeated but their leader, Saddam Hussein, was still at large. Because the leader—Satan—is at large, he can still cause a tremendous amount of damage. The war is over but we still have to apply the victory over the devil Jesus won for us.

THE WEAPONS OF OUR WARFARE

YOU MAY BE "GOD'S RAMBO," taking on the powers of hell, exercising the authority of Jesus, but unless you have the right weapons, it is an exercise in futility. Paul writes, "For though we walk in the flesh, we do not war after the flesh" (2 Cor. 10:3). The weapons we use aren't F-16s or AK-47s. They're not fleshly, natural, carnal weapons that can be held or touched. "(For the weapons of our warfare are not carnal, but mighty through God to the pulling down of strongholds;) Casting down imaginations, and every high thing that exalteth itself against the knowledge of God, and bringing into captivity every thought to the obedience of Christ" (2 Cor. 10:4–5). Think about this: The focus of our battle centers on imaginations and everything that exalts itself against the knowledge of God, with the end result being to bring every thought into captivity to the obedience of Christ. The battle we fight dwells in the realm of thoughts, ideas, and imaginations.

THE BELIEVER'S JOB DESCRIPTION

WE HAVE A TREMENDOUS ASSIGNMENT before us. Paul writes, "For we wrestle not against flesh and blood, but against principalities, against powers, against the rulers of the darkness of this world, against spiritual wickedness in high places" (Eph. 6:12). Most Christians stop at the phrase "For we wrestle not." They say to themselves, "We ain't gonna wrestle." The fact of the matter is, if you refuse to wrestle, you're just going to get yourself pinned down. When you refuse to wrestle, you settle for whatever life—or the enemy—hands you.

The believer doesn't wrestle against people with bodies. The battle isn't with your husband, your wife, or your employer. It's against principalities and powers—evil spirit beings that use, inhabit, come upon, or motivate people with bodies to do wrong things. God is telling us that our battle is against those principalities and powers that raise up strongholds—those influences that motivate people to act contrary to the Word of God.

THE BATTLEFIELD OF THE MIND

PAUL SAYS OUR WEAPONS ARE MIGHTY for the pulling down of strongholds. Whose strongholds are these? Satan's. Where are the strongholds? In the realm of the mind. What are these strongholds, or fortresses, that Satan builds in people's minds? It's the inability or refusal to comprehend God's truth. Basically the strongholds are prejudices—making your mind up before you get all the facts. You've heard the statement, "Don't confuse me with facts; I've got my mind made up." That's a stronghold.

Take, for example, the Jehovah's Witnesses. You can discuss and explain what the Word of God really says about their aberrant beliefs all day long, and they still won't hear a word you're saying. Jesus referred to such people as those who have eyes that don't see and ears that don't hear (Matt. 13:14). People like this have hardened hearts. Their inability to comprehend what the Word of God says is a sign of a stronghold or fortress.

A stronghold resides in the person who thinks he is beyond the forgiveness of Jesus Christ. Perhaps even after becoming a Christian, he committed a sin that he believes God is unable to forgive. He may read in 1 John 1:9 that Jesus "is faithful and just to forgive our sins, and to cleanse us from all unrighteousness," but refuse to believe that it applies to him. Thus, every day he walks in defeat.

A stronghold resides in the person who, when confronted with his bondage to a spirit of Jezebel or Lucifer, refuses to accept correction from God's appointed authority in the church.

A stronghold resides in any system of belief that sets itself up against the knowledge of God. Communism is a stronghold because it begins with the premise that God is an invention of the human imagination. Even Capitalism has inherent strongholds because its basis of motivation is greed. A stronghold is any belief that sets itself in opposition to the knowledge of God and deafens the ears of its adherents to the truth of God's Word and the voice of the Holy Spirit.

We have a tremendous assignment from God if we're

going to participate in seeing people won into the kingdom. Our responsibility is to break down the strongholds in peoples' minds that prevent them from receiving the gospel of salvation. God wants us to release the minds of people from captivity to Satan and bring their minds into captivity and obedience to Christ Jesus.

THE ONLY PEOPLE EQUIPPED TO INTERVENE

PEOPLE BOUGHT BY THE BLOOD OF JESUS CHRIST and knowledgeable in the weapons of their warfare are the only group on earth equipped to intervene in the spiritual realm. Christians who don't know how to use their weapons, or who refuse or neglect them, are stuck in the crossfire between good and evil. Where would you rather be during a battle—on one side shooting at the enemy *or in the middle dodging bullets from either side?* Christians who refuse to participate in the battle are the ones most likely to live in defeat. Not only are they satisfied with so much less of God's best but they model to the world a powerless, impotent gospel.

Jesus spoke candidly to the church in Laodicea saying, "So, because you are lukewarm—neither hot nor cold—I am about to spit you out of my mouth" (Rev. 3:16, NIV). We are the most significant people on the face of the earth, but the trouble is, we don't act like it because we don't really know and believe it.

Because the battle we fight is not political but spiritual, we have the answer and the weapons to stop it—the answer is not the military, not the politicians. It's as if the whole universe were screaming, "Wake up, church! Wake up to your destiny and to your heritage. Do something."

The Nature of Spiritual Warfare

THE FULL ARMOR

BEFORE LISTING THE WEAPONS OF BATTLE in Ephesians 6, Paul prefaces his explanation with a piece of advice: "Therefore put on the full armor of God, so that when the day of evil comes, you may be able to stand your ground, and after you have done everything, to stand" (Eph. 6:13, NIV). Twice in Ephesians 6, Paul exhorts the believer to put on the full armor of God. In the Greek language, *full armor* is denoted by only one word—*panoplia*—from which we derive the English word *panoply*. A panoply refers to the complete arms and armor of a warrior. A panoply denotes a single unit of armor. The warrior doesn't wear only pieces of armor that are comfortable or convenient because without the full panoply, the warrior is less than effective and susceptible to injury.

Paul continues by explaining what the panoply—the full armor—is:

> Stand therefore, having your loins girt about with truth, and having on the breastplate of righteousness; And your feet shod with the preparation of the gospel of peace; Above all, taking the shield of faith, wherewith ye shall be able to quench all the fiery darts of the wicked. And take the helmet of salvation, and the sword of the Spirit, which is the word of God: Praying always with all prayer and supplication in the Spirit, and watching thereunto with all perseverance and supplication for all saints.
>
> —Ephesians 6:14–18

It is important to understand the function of each piece of armor. Let's take a brief look at each piece:

The belt of truth

The first item of use to the warrior in God's army is the belt of truth. The belt of truth holds everything together. It keeps the breastplate in position, the garment in place, and it also holds the sword. The belt of truth represents the believer's integrity and faithfulness. In one word: obedience. No person is perfect, and our right relationship with God comes through the blood of Jesus, but we still must enter the battle with integrity. Sin that we refuse to deal with or that we cover up will make us vulnerable to the enemy. But with truth come freedom, ease of movement, and confidence.

The breastplate of righteousness

The breastplate of righteousness *covers the heart,* the most vital organ. The heart is the seat of our emotions, feelings, passions—it is the reflection of who we really are. If Satan can affect our heart, we can be easily defeated. Satan accuses us of every misdeed, every wrong motive, anything he can use to neutralize us. As Christians, we walk in the righteousness that comes not from our good works but from what Christ accomplished on the cross. *That is why Satan tries so hard to obscure the cross.* If he succeeds in obscuring the cross of Christ, it is tantamount to removing our breastplate of righteousness.

Notice that the belt of truth—or integrity—and the breastplate of righteousness work together. Without the breastplate of righteousness, we operate in legalism. Without the belt of truth, we operate in carnality and the flesh.

The Nature of Spiritual Warfare

The shoes of the preparation of the gospel of peace

The shoes represent *peace of mind*. In the heat of battle, the greatest temptation the warrior faces is that of growing fearful and retreating. Our foundation in the gospel will keep us from turning away and exposing our vulnerable backside to the onslaught of the enemy. Notice the word *preparation*. The battle actually begins before the conflict. You can't cram for a battle like you can for a test in school. Our preparation of standing on the Word of God begins *before* the conflict arises. Once the battle is raging it's too late to prepare.

The shield of faith

The purpose of the shield is to protect the other parts of the armor and to absorb the fiery arrows of the enemy. Our *faith in God*—our response to what Christ accomplished on the cross for us—extinguishes the fiery arrows of Satan's accusations and lies. The breastplate of righteousness comes from God. The shield of faith is our response, our belief, to what Christ accomplished for us on Calvary.

The helmet of salvation

What does the helmet of salvation protect? *The mind.* Notice Paul says, "Take the helmet" meaning to put it on. In fact, Paul states this as a command: "Take the helmet and put it on." If you're saved, isn't the helmet automatically on? No. Why would he tell the Ephesians Christians to put it on if it's already on?

Paul, in 1 Thessalonians 5:8, refers to the helmet as the hope of salvation. Faith protects my heart; "For with the heart man believeth" (Rom. 10:10). But hope protects my mind against discouragement and depression.

Hope is in the realm of the mind. So Paul admonishes us to put on our helmets. Cultivate a positive attitude. Why? Romans 8:28 says, "And we know that all things work together for good to them that love God, to them who are the called according to his purpose." If I love God, and I'm walking in His purpose for me, then anything that God allows to happen, whether the devil brings it or God sends it, is for my good. When I'm walking in covenant, there's not a reason in the world to be unhappy or depressed about any setback.

Walking in the hope of salvation is conditional. As long as I love God and walk in obedience, when all hell breaks loose, I will not be cast down and depressed because I haven't done anything wrong. God's making the best of it, even if it's sent by the enemy.

The Christian can, however, refuse to put on the helmet. As a result that person is weak, impotent, and powerless. But when we walk in the hope of our salvation, we're in a no-lose situation. Paul said, "For whether we live, we live unto the Lord; and whether we die, we die unto the Lord: whether we live therefore, or die, we are the Lord's" (Rom. 14:8).

Take Joseph for example: He was mistreated, sold into bondage by his brothers, separated from his family, falsely accused of attempted rape, imprisoned, and forgotten while in jail. God gave him a dream as a boy that someday he would be a man of influence, and yet the best years of his life were being wasted away in prison! His life seemed pretty depressing for a person who was supposed to have a big destiny. But Joseph cultivated a positive attitude. Even while in prison, he made the best of his situation, rising to second in command over the prison where he was held captive.

Joseph never gave up hope, and eventually God rewarded his faithfulness. In Genesis 50, in the presence of his brothers who sold him into slavery, Joseph looked them right in the eyes and said, "You intended to harm me, but God intended it for good" (Gen. 50:20, NIV). Joseph had every right to have his brothers killed, but he saw his life from God's perspective. He refused to allow bitterness and depression to take root in his life because he knew if they did, he would miss out on God's destiny for his life. Joseph saw his life through the helmet of salvation.

That's why children need encouragement when they leave for school. If they have a negative spirit before they take a test, the parent needs to respond with, "No, you're not going to do bad on that test; you have studied well. The Spirit of God is upon you; I've prayed for you. You're going to do very well, and I bless you." Put the helmet on them!

If your accountant comes to you and says, "I've got bad news for you; you owe the IRS more than I expected!" you can put on the helmet of salvation and reply, "Thank You, Lord! I praise You. It's for my good and blessing. I don't understand; it doesn't make any sense to me in the natural, but I know You meant it for good. And I give You praise that You're going to supply the extra money I'm going to have to pay this year. Thank You!"

You put on the helmet every time you act upon the knowledge that God is orchestrating events. *It's hard to be negative when you know God is in control.*

God is in control even when ungodly and evil leaders are corrupting an entire nation. God raises up bad kings as well as good kings. There is no person in political office whom God hasn't placed there by His divine power. No one. Daniel proclaimed that "the Most High is sovereign over the kingdoms of men and gives them to anyone he wishes and sets over them the lowliest of men" (Dan. 4:17, NIV). Knowing that God is in total control keeps me from being negative and defeated when life doesn't go the way I think it ought to. Our positive attitude and hope in God then becomes a helmet of salvation.

The sword of the Spirit

The final implement in the spiritual armor is the sword of the Spirit, which is the *Word of God*. The first five weapons are defensive weapons, but the sword is used as an offensive weapon. The Holy Spirit's main weapon is the Word of God. Notice Paul says, "the sword of the Spirit, which is the word of God" (Eph. 6:17). The Word of God belongs to the Holy Spirit. When Jesus was tempted in the wilderness, three times He responded by using His offensive weapon—the Word of God. And we already know what happened—the devil departed.

The writer of Hebrews likens the Word of God to a sword: "For the word of God is living and active. Sharper than any double-edged sword, it penetrates even to dividing soul and spirit, joints and marrow; it judges the thoughts and attitudes of the heart" (Heb. 4:12, NIV). You may have read one of the classic, timeless pieces of literature—it may be your favorite book—but it is still dead—its author is dead, and it has no ability to change lives. But the Holy Spirit uses the Word of God to change lives today just as it changed lives two thousand years ago. Through the power of the Holy Spirit, the Word of God is able to transform a person and breathe life into a cold, lifeless spirit.

The Word of God penetrates "even to the dividing asunder of soul and spirit"—it is able to judge what comes from the arm of the flesh and what is truly of God (Heb. 4:12). The Word of God divides joints and marrow. In ancient times, the bone marrow represented the true nature of a person—that place that no one else could see. You cannot get any more hidden than the bone marrow in a person's body. The Word of God penetrates into the very essence of who a person is, judging the thoughts and attitudes of the heart. Only two people really know your true thoughts and attitudes—you and God. When we use the sword of the Spirit, it often works at levels that the soldier cannot see.

PRAYING IN THE SPIRIT: A WEAPON

THE SWORD CAN REACH ONLY AS FAR as the arm can extend, which is why Paul continues in his explanation of the armor, "Praying always with all prayer and supplication in the Spirit." While my sword is limited to the measure of my arm's reach, prayer is limitless. It's like an intercontinental ballistic missile. I can launch it from South Africa, and it will impact anywhere in the world. You can launch a prayer right now, and you can send that missile of the Word worldwide and not have to be there. When we pray in the Spirit—in tongues—we are able to pray specifically into a situation we may know nothing about.

Mike inquired through his travel agent about flying to Munich as soon as possible, only to discover that all flights from the local airport were booked. Undeterred in his efforts and against his inner witness, he decided to travel to London where he was able to get a flight out of Heathrow Airport.

As the aircraft took off, Mike watched the clouds from his window seat as the plane climbed up to ten thousand feet. Suddenly he noticed a little black dot on the horizon that appeared to be coming toward his plane. As the dot grew larger, Mike realized that it was another plane possibly traveling at the same altitude and in his direction! It was closing in too fast for his plane to change either direction or altitude so soon after take off.

For a split second, Mike thought he was going to die. His whole life passed before him. He pulled himself together as he confessed the scripture which says that no weapon formed against him would prosper. He rebuked fear, and pleaded the blood of Jesus over the plane he was traveling in.

Hearing this, the passenger sitting next to Mike got up and hurried to another seat. As Mike prayed in tongues, his plane made a sudden left turn downward. When Mike looked out the window, he noticed the other plane passing overhead—so close that he could see the pilots in the other plane and the rivets in the plane's underbelly! The power of prayer had averted a mid-air collision.

God has prepared us for battle by equipping us with our spiritual panoply—the armor we need. Putting on the armor of God is essential in prevailing over the powers of the enemy in battle. In the next chapter we will learn *how* to use it.

Nine

LAUNCHING OUR WEAPONS

MMUNITION IS USELESS WITHOUT SOMETHING to launch it. A bullet needs a gun; an arrow needs a bow. A bomb needs a bomber plane to drop it. There are three spiritual weapons, or means, to launch our ammunition against Satan's kingdom: The Word of God, the blood of Jesus, and the name of Jesus. We have explored the basis for using the blood of Jesus. We have studied the use of our weapons and the Word. In this chapter we look at the power in the name of Jesus.

The name of Jesus, even today, throws the supernatural world into disorder. It's a name often abused by the world, yet when it is expressed in godly power, its impact is felt by saint and sinner alike. It is at the name of Jesus that every knee will bow and every tongue will confess that Jesus Christ is Lord (Phil. 2:10–11). Satan knows that eventually he will have to bow his knee to Jesus, and the thought makes him cringe! He will do whatever he can to avoid hearing the name of Jesus.

The Bible tells us we are saved through confessing Jesus as Lord: "That if thou shalt confess with thy mouth the Lord Jesus, and shalt believe in thine heart that God hath raised him from the dead, thou shalt be saved. For with the heart man believeth unto righteousness; and with the mouth confession is made unto salvation" (Rom. 10:9–10).

We are baptized in the name of Jesus: "Then Peter said unto them, Repent, and be baptized every one of you in the name of Jesus Christ, for the remission of sins, and ye shall receive the gift of the Holy Ghost" (Acts 2:38).

We speak healing in the name of Jesus: "Then Peter said, Silver and gold have I none; but such as I have give I thee: In the name of Jesus Christ of Nazareth rise up and walk" (Acts 3:6).

And we are able to cast out demons in the name of Jesus: "But Paul, being grieved, turned and said to the spirit, I command thee in the name of Jesus Christ to come out of her. And he came out the same hour" (Acts 16:18). In the nineteenth chapter of Acts, the seven sons of Sceva attempted to cast demons out of certain individuals. Because they weren't Christians the demons responded, "Jesus I know, and Paul I know; but who are ye?" (Acts 19:15). Then an evil spirit came after them!

The Jewish authorities ordered Peter and John not to teach in the name of Jesus because it caused riots in Jerusalem (Acts 4:18). Whenever Paul and John taught about Jesus, it spurred extreme reactions among the people—mostly in opposition because he upset their understanding of the law. But on a deeper level, it also threw the principalities and powers into an upheaval.

It's interesting to note the frequency at which the name of Jesus is used in the Book of Acts compared to other New Testament books. Eighteen times in the Book of Acts the name of Jesus is used as a weapon, compared with only two times in all four Gospels. For the early church, the name of Jesus was an important weapon in the battle against Satan. The Book of Acts is a window into the everyday life of the New Testament church and a model for how the church should operate today. Through it we see how the early believers dealt with struggles, successes, and spirits. There is power in the mere mention of the name of Jesus.

FOUR LAUNCHING PADS

THE WEAPONS OF OUR WARFARE HAVE FOUR launching pads: prayer, preaching, praise, and testimony. These launching pads are only effective if they're loaded with the Word of God, the name of Jesus, and the blood of Jesus.

1. *Prayer.* Prayer launches our ammunition against the enemy. This was explained in the previous chapter. Through prayer we can extend beyond what is within arms reach.

2. *Preaching.* The word preach means "to proclaim." The goal of preaching is to proclaim what God has accomplished through Jesus Christ. Paul rightly asked the church in Rome, "How then shall they call on him in whom they have not believed? and how shall they believe in him of whom they have not heard? and how shall they hear without a preacher?" (Rom. 10:14). It is in hearing the preached Word that we understand and know the power in God's Word.

Everywhere Paul went, he preached about the blood of Jesus. He wrote to the church in Corinth, "But we preach Christ crucified, unto the Jews a stumbling block, and unto the Greeks foolishness . . . And I was with you in weakness, and in fear, and in much trembling. And my speech and my preaching was not with enticing words of man's wisdom, but in demonstration of the Spirit and of power" (1 Cor. 1:23; 2:3–4). Paul preached with power because he proclaimed the blood of Jesus. Satan obscures the cross to rob the gospel of its power.

3. *Praise.* If you were in a room where people spent all their time praising Satan, what would you want to do? You would have two choices: Either get the people to stop, or leave the room. Satan faces the same dilemma. Either he will do whatever he can to stop you, or he has no choice but to leave the area.

Even small children can "preach" or proclaim God's victory—launching an attack against Satan. The psalmist writes in Psalm 8:2, "Out of the mouth of *babes* and sucklings hast thou [God] ordained strength because of thine enemies, that thou mightest still the enemy and the avenger" (Ps. 8:2, italics added). Who is the enemy and the avenger? It is Satan. Jesus interprets this passage in Matthew 21 by saying:

And when the chief priests and scribes saw the wonderful things that he did . . . they were sore displeased, And said unto him, Hearest thou what these say? And Jesus saith

106

unto them, Yea; have ye never read, Out of
the mouth of *babes* and sucklings thou hast
perfected praise?
　　　　　　—Matthew 21:15–16, italics added

Why is it important to silence Satan? Because he's
constantly accusing us. He stands before God all day
long casting blame on us for every action, misdeed—
anything he can find—that will heap guilt and
condemnation on us. Twenty-four hours a day, seven
days a week, Satan accuses us before the Father. "And I
heard a loud voice saying in heaven, Now is come salvation, and strength, and the kingdom of our God, and
the power of his Christ: for the accuser of our brethren
is cast down, *which accused them before our God day
and night*" (Rev. 12:10, italics added). Satan accused
Job before the Father (Job 1:6–9), and he accused Jesus
before the Father (Zech. 3:1). What is the purpose of
his accusation? To inflict guilt and condemnation.

We impose silence on the enemy through praise.
When you praise God, you open up the divine lines of
communication. You can hear God communing with
you, and you with Him. Why? Because the distractions
are gone. The enemy is silenced through perfected
praise.

4. *The word of your testimony.* The last
launching pad to overcome Satan is the
word of your testimony. "And they"—the
ones being accused—"overcame him"—
Satan—"by the blood of the Lamb, and by
the word of their testimony; and they loved
not their lives unto the death" (Rev. 12:11).

In the Christian's arsenal of weapons, we
have the Word of God and the word of our
testimony. The word of our testimony is the

evidence of the Word of God in our lives. The words *accusation* and *testimony* are legal terms from a court of law. The word *accusation* gives the idea of a prosecuting attorney accusing the defendant of a specific crime. In response, the defendant presents their *testimony* of innocence.

As believers, we can testify that through the shed blood of Jesus Christ, our accuser has no basis to level blame because our record is clean. We have been washed anew by the blood of Jesus. If Satan is successful in obscuring the work of the cross in our lives, then he can water down our testimony.

We overcome Satan when we testify to what the Word of God says about the blood of Jesus and what that blood has done for us. But to do that, we have to know what the Word says about the blood of Jesus. When we fail to know what the Word of God says, we are destined for defeat.

When Satan tries to work guilt or condemnation into our lives from the sins of our past, we can respond with the Word of God in prayer by saying, "Satan, in the name of Jesus, you cannot bring the sins of my past upon me because 1 John 1:7 tells me that the blood of Jesus purifies me from *all* sin."

AFFIRMATIONS TO DEFEAT SATAN

WE KNOW THAT BECAUSE SATAN IS the accuser of the brethren, he *will* accuse us. It's not a question of *if* he will do so, it is *when*. When he does accuse us, we can use the following statements as weapons to overcome Satan's accusations.

Launching Our Weapons

1. In Christ we have redemption through His blood.

"IN WHOM [CHRIST] WE HAVE REDEMPTION through his blood, the forgiveness of sins, according to the riches of his grace" (Eph. 1:7). It's not a result of our works but through the blood of Jesus that we are forgiven. *Redemption* means "to buy back." Through the first Adam, we sold ourselves as slaves to sin, but Jesus came to the pawn shop and bought us back. He redeemed us. Whenever something is redeemed, it costs more to buy it back than it does to sell it. When you hock something at a pawn shop, they give you twenty-five dollars; but to buy back it might cost a hundred fifty dollars. Jesus was the only person who could claim your pawn ticket because He was the only perfect, sinless human being. He was the only one who could buy you back because it required sinless, innocent blood. *Through the blood of Jesus I am redeemed out of the hand of the devil.*

2. Through the blood we are continually cleansed from sin.

"BUT IF WE WALK IN THE LIGHT, as he is in the light, we have fellowship one with another, and the blood of Jesus Christ his Son cleanseth us from all sin" (1 John 1:7). The word *cleanseth* in Greek gives the idea of a continual cleansing. Now bear in mind this cleansing process is contingent upon whether or not we are walking in the light. If we are not walking in the light the blood is not cleansing us. If we live our lives in such a way that we open ourselves up to the conviction of the Holy Spirit, and respond to that conviction, the blood of Jesus cleanses us now and continually from all sin.

Through the blood of Jesus, while I'm walking in the light, the blood of Jesus is cleansing me now and continually from all sin.

3. Through the blood we are made righteous.

"MUCH MORE THEN, being now *justified* by his blood, we shall be saved from wrath through him" (Rom. 5:9, italics added). The word *justified* is another legal term meaning "acquitted" or "made righteous." A person who is acquitted of a crime has the legal right to avoid the penalty of that offense—even if they actually committed the crime. Society says, "Commit the crime, do the time." Because we are born in sin, we acknowledge that we have committed the crime, but because of the blood of Jesus, we don't have to do the time in hell. So we can say, *through the blood of Jesus I am justified, acquitted, not guilty, reckoned righteous, and made righteous—just as if I have never sinned.*

4. Through the blood we are partakers in God's holiness.

"THEREFORE JESUS ALSO, that He might sanctify the people through His own blood, suffered outside the gate" (Heb. 13:12, NAS). The word *sanctify* means to be made holy. Because God is holy, He cannot look at sin. When Jesus was hanging on the cross, He cried out "My God, My God, why have you forsaken me?" (Matt. 27:46, NIV). The reason why Jesus sensed a separation from God's presence while on the cross was because at that moment, He bore the sins of the world in His body. By the blood of Jesus, we are set apart from sin and made partakers of God's holiness. With this benefit, we have the right to come boldly before the throne of grace and spend eternity with our heavenly Father. So through the blood of Jesus I can say I am sanctified, made holy, set apart from sin and Satan's kingdom, and made a partaker in God's holiness. We thank God for His goodness, we praise God for His greatness, but we worship Him for His holiness.

When Satan tries to bring us under guilt and condemnation, we respond to him with the Word of God, the name of Jesus, and the blood of Jesus through prayer, praise, preaching, and the word of our testimony.

PART III

THE POWER OF THE CROSS IN THE LIFE OF THE BELIEVER

Ten

DELIVERANCE
FROM THE LAW

N THIS LAST DIVISION OF THE BOOK, I will give you a
window into seeing the power of the cross in the
life of the believer—free from the influences of
witchcraft. There are three benefits of the cross
in the life of the believer. The first operation or benefit
of the cross in the life of the believer is deliverance
from the law. We've already dealt with the problem of
legalism in the church; now let's see what freedom
from legalism looks like in the life of the believer.

Paul says, "For I through the Law [under the operation of the curse of the Law] have [in Christ's death for
me] myself died to the Law and all the Law's demands
upon me, so that I may [henceforth] live to and for God"
(Gal. 2:19, AMP). When did I die to the law? When Christ
died. Our old man was crucified with Jesus when He

died on the cross. So through the cross and the death of Jesus two thousand years ago, I already died to the law.

The law—legalism—causes our sinful passions to come alive. "For when we were controlled by the sinful nature, the sinful passions aroused by the law were at work in our bodies, so that we bore fruit for death. But now, by dying to what once bound us, we have been released [or delivered] from the law so that we serve in the new way of the Spirit, and not in the old way of the written code" (Rom. 7:5–6, NIV).

When you were a child, did you ever have a time when you were told not to do something, and because you were told not to do it, you did it? Because of our sin nature, being told not to do something is often all the incentive we need to do that very thing—oftentimes for no other reason than just because we were told not to do it! The more laws you have, the easier it is to be a law-breaker. In fact, the law works as a deterrent to true obedience because the law is devoid of a connection to a relationship. But those who consider themselves to have died with Christ have been released from the law. Those who are in Christ are no longer under the law; the incentive for doing right and not doing wrong is based on a relationship with Jesus Christ.

ONLY DEATH CAN RELEASE US FROM THE LAW

THE ONLY WAY TO BE RELEASED from the law is through death:

> Do you not know, brothers—for I am speaking to men who know the law—that the law has authority over a man only as long as he lives? For example, by law a married woman is bound to her husband as long as he is alive, but if her husband dies, she is released from the law of marriage. So

then, if she marries another man while her husband is still alive, she is called an adulteress. But if her husband dies, she is released from that law and is not an adulteress, even though she marries another man.

So, my brothers, you also died to the law through the body of Christ, that you might belong to another, to him who was raised from the dead, in order that we might bear fruit to God.

—Romans 7:1–4, NIV

It is by the law that we were married to our carnal nature, and the fruit produced out of that union were the works of the flesh. The good news is this: On the cross that carnal nature died in Jesus.

The only way to be totally released from a marriage is through death. Because of our relationship to the first Adam, we were married to sin and the law. But through our death with Christ on the cross, we're freed from our "marriage" to sin and the law. Now we're free to "marry" someone else. We're freed from that law; we don't have to go back to that evil marriage partner because the law died with Christ on the cross. We have a new marriage partner, the Lord Jesus.

That's why, at the end of the age, Jesus isn't going to marry the unbelieving, apostate Israel. Because He died, He's free from His covenant relationship to the law and Israel; the church is now His bride. Paul calls God's new covenantal chosen people the Israel of God: "Neither circumcision nor uncircumcision means anything; what counts is a new creation. Peace and mercy to all who follow this rule, even to the Israel of God" (Gal. 6:15–16, NIV).

The Israel of God is chosen not by physical birth as in the Old Covenant but by new birth in Christ Jesus. People in the Israel of God come regardless of color or

117

ethnicity and operate on the basis of a personal relationship with Jesus Christ—something that under the Old Covenant Israel couldn't do.

THE KEY: UNION WITH CHRIST

THERE ARE TWO POSSIBLE UNIONS. One, you can be united with your fleshly nature and the law. The fruit of that union are the works of the flesh:

> So I say, live by the Spirit, and you will not gratify the desires of the sinful nature. For the sinful nature desires what is contrary to the Spirit, and the Spirit what is contrary to the sinful nature. They are in conflict with each other, so that you do not do what you want. But if you are led by the Spirit, you are not under law.
>
> The acts of the sinful nature are obvious: sexual immorality, impurity and debauchery; idolatry and witchcraft; hatred, discord, jealousy, fits of rage, selfish ambition, dissensions, factions and envy; drunkenness, orgies, and the like. I warn you, as I did before, that those who live like this will not inherit the kingdom of God.
>
> —Galatians 5:16–21, NIV

That's the marriage under the law.

The second possible union is marriage to Christ. The Israel of God is married to the resurrected Christ, and the result of that union is the fruit of the Spirit:

> But the fruit of the Spirit is love, joy, peace, patience, kindness, goodness, faithfulness, gentleness and self-control. Against such things there is no law.
>
> —Galatians 5:22–23, NIV

We do not automatically produce the fruit of the Spirit. Christianity is not a religion of doing your best. You didn't come to Christ by first doing good. Many people believe they have to get their act together *before* they come to God. Jesus, however, said, "It is not the healthy who need a doctor, but the sick. I have not come to call the righteous, but sinners to repentance" (Luke 5:31–32, NIV). Jesus calls those who acknowledge their need to come to Him first.

After our marriage to Christ, He then works with us on the details of our lives. The focus, however, is our union to Christ—our relationship. We will produce the fruit of that union as we develop the relationship, becoming more and more like our marriage partner. Sadly, the same is true for the person who is united to the law and to a fleshly nature. That person will also produce more and more of the fruit of the flesh.

In John 15, Jesus spoke about the vine and the branches, "I am the true vine, and my Father is the gardener . . . Remain in me, and I will remain in you. No branch can bear fruit by itself; it must remain in the vine. Neither can you bear fruit unless you remain in me. I am the vine; you are the branches. If a man remains in me and I in him, he will bear much fruit; apart from me you can do nothing" (vv. 1, 4–5, NIV). Our Heavenly Father is the gardener, Jesus is the vine, and we—the church—are the branches. The sap or the life source in the vine is the Holy Spirit. When the branch abides in the vine, does the vine get out there and say, "Come on, guys! We have to produce some fruit today. Let's hump it up; let's get a good blossom going! God's going to be out here in the garden in a little bit to look at us. Let's work it up and try to blossom"?

No. Life flows into the branches simply because they are connected to the vine. It's not a matter of trying, it's a matter of union. By being grafted into Jesus, the true vine, we're going to produce His life. When His life is flowing into us, it has to produce life in us, and out of that life, obedience comes naturally.

People are fearful of relationships based on union and not the law. "Oh, Lord! We'll just go off and do whatever we want." No, you will not. If a person is in union with the Holy Spirit, he will not be led into sin: "When tempted, no one should say, 'God is tempting me.' For God cannot be tempted by evil, nor does he tempt anyone" (James 1:13, NIV). Our goal should be to get people in union with Christ.

Paul wrote to Timothy that the goal of their mentoring relationship and specifically of the letter he was writing, was "love, which comes from a pure heart and a good conscience and a sincere faith" (1 Tim. 1:5, NIV). Paul sought to build in Timothy a relationship of love based not on rules—the exterior things we see—but based on heart issues; something that the naked eye cannot see and the law cannot touch or monitor. If we are in union with Christ and led by the Spirit, if the rule is right, God will lead us to obey that rule. But our right standing with God still isn't dependent on whether or not we kept that rule. Most people feel uncomfortable with that. It relies too much on God and not enough on what we can do ourselves. But that's the way God likes it. It's all of God and none of me.

THE RESULT OF UNION WITH THE LAW: WITCHCRAFT

BUT IF WE'RE IN UNION WITH THE LAW, we open ourselves up to witchcraft which is displayed through manipulation, domination, and intimidation. We try to make people do things that should be birthed out of a relationship. In a home, parents may be strict and unmerciful with their children. In the workplace, a legalistic person may do everything "by the book" without any trace of mercy, compassion, or feeling.

In the church, a legalistic person may get upset over insignificant issues, distracting the church from her mission. People with a Lucifer or Jezebel spirit love legalism because it presents the opportunity to point out flaws in the authority structure of a church. I'm always leery of people who point out the flaws in others because I know those flaws may very well be the issues they are struggling with in their own lives. And what is the fruit of their legalism? Death. That's why fruit-producing is a matter of union, not effort.

THE RESULTS OF DELIVERANCE FROM THE LAW

THERE ARE SEVERAL RESULTS THAT can be seen in the lives of people who have been delivered from the law.

Freedom from condemnation

First of all, deliverance from the law brings freedom from condemnation. "Therefore, there is now no condemnation for those who are in Christ Jesus, because through Christ Jesus the law of the Spirit of life set me free from the law of sin and death" (Rom. 8:1–2, NIV). The Spirit that gives life frees us from the law that brings death. Later on in the same chapter, Paul asks the crucial question: "Who will bring any charge against those whom God has chosen? It is God who justifies. Who is he that condemns?" (Rom. 8:33–34, NIV). Because it is God who justifies us in Christ Jesus, there is no one who can level an honest claim to condemn us. When we are in Christ Jesus, our record is clean.

Freedom to love

Second, we're free to love. Legalism and love produce opposing results. Legalists get mean. They criticize and judge everything. Paul, however, writes, "Owe no man any thing, but to love one another: for he that loveth another hath fulfilled the law" (Rom. 13:8). If you don't love, but you're keeping all the rules, you haven't fulfilled anything but your flesh. If you love one another you've fulfilled the law.

The first four commandments address our relationship with God. The last six commandments—"honour thy father and thy mother, thou shalt not commit adultery, thou shalt not kill, thou shalt not steal, thou shalt not bear false witness, thou shalt not covet"—can all be summed up in one simple command: *Love your neighbor as yourself.* When Jesus was asked what was the greatest commandment, He answered with two commandments: "'Love the Lord your God with all your heart and with all your soul and with all your mind'. . . . And the second is like it: 'Love your neighbor as yourself'" (Matt. 22:37, 39, NIV). We first love God— we're in union with Christ through the Holy Spirit. The result of that union is love for one's neighbor. These two commandments sum up the spirit of the Old Testament law.

When a person walks in love, the law is unnecessary. If I love you, I'm not going to steal from you, or hurt you, or slander you. Laws are for the law breaker—the criminal—not the righteous (1 Tim. 1:9). So when I operate in love, I don't need the law. People operating under the law find their ability to love is limited. But when you work in the opposite direction of legalism, you find yourself free to love.

When you're bound by the law your carnal nature produces everything *but* good fruit: hate, jealousy, selfishness, division, lasciviousness, adultery. When you're bound by the law, your first response to actions of other people is to see which particular law has been violated by these people.

When you are in union with the source of love, you bear the fruit of the Spirit. John even writes that "God is love" (1 John 4:16). The character of God is represented in the fruit of the Spirit. When Paul lists the fruit of the Spirit in Galatians 5:22–23, he begins with love. It is a commonly held belief among students of the Bible that the sum total of the fruit of the Spirit represent love. Like an orange with eight wedges, the eight wedges of that fruit of love are joy, peace, patience, kindness, goodness, faithfulness, gentleness, and self-control. As we remain in union with Christ, the result of that union is a self-sacrificing love which expresses itself through the fruit of the Spirit.

Freedom to be led by the Holy Spirit

The third benefit of being delivered from the law is the freedom to be led by the Holy Spirit. "But if you are led by the Spirit, you are not under law" (Gal. 5:18, NIV). If you are not under the law it doesn't mean that you are automatically led by the Spirit, but it does mean you have the freedom to be led by the Spirit. This verse does tell us that you cannot be led by the Spirit and be under the law at the same time. So if you want to be led by the Spirit, you have to come out from under the law. If you have difficulty sensing the presence and leading of the Holy Spirit, it may mean that you are still operating under the law.

Haven't we as believers said so many times, "I'll make it; I can do it myself," not realizing that we're grieving the Holy Spirit and pushing Him away. We try to improve ourselves, but we try to do it by using the arm of the flesh: "I'll be a better person; I won't do that again; I won't have an affair again; I won't smoke again."

Recently, our family discontinued our subscription to a movie channel on cable television. It doesn't make everybody stumble, but it was a potential stumbling block for me, so I took it out. That's not law. The Bible says, "make no provision for the flesh to fulfill its lusts" (Rom. 14:13). God impressed upon me that sometimes at night when I'm tired, I turn the TV on and subject myself to movies that blemish me. But it wasn't condemnation. The Holy Spirit told me, "Why don't you just call down to the movie channel and cut it off, then you won't have to fool with it." I was being led by the Spirit, not by the law. I didn't sense any condemnation, guilt, or shame. And it's wonderful; I don't miss it at all. Now I have more time to read and more time to study. It didn't control me; it's just a little area, a bridge that the enemy was using to try to make an entrance into my life.

It isn't limited to television. For some people it may be the friends they keep or the places they go. It's different in everybody's life. The key is listening to the Holy Spirit. He's not out to destroy me. When the Spirit speaks, His voice is sweet and soft. We're brought into a right relationship with God not by rules but by being led by the Holy Spirit.

THE TRUE MEASURE OF SUCCESS

CHARLES FINNEY SAID THE GAUGE of a minister's success is the measure of the Holy Spirit in his ministry. When Jesus entered the Jordan River to be baptized, John the Baptist pronounced, "Behold the Lamb of God, which taketh away the sin of the world" (John 1:29). Following His subsequent baptism, the heavens opened and the Holy Spirit, in the form of a dove, settled on Jesus' head. The Holy Spirit rested on the Lamb of God. Now a dove is a fretful, little bird; it's clean and picky about where it sits down. The Holy Spirit is the same way. He won't rest on you if there's anger, strife, or something that will frighten Him. The Holy Spirit chose to rest upon the Lamb of God, the Lord Jesus, just as He will choose to rest upon the believer whose life is filled with Christ.

The character of that Lamb was threefold: purity, meekness, and a life sacrificially laid down. If you want the Holy Spirit to lead you in power, you're going to have to ask the Holy Spirit to give you the quality and character of the Lamb so He'll rest on you and lead you.

Because legalism is based in control, the opposite of legalism is freedom. "It is for freedom that Christ has redeemed us" (Gal. 5:1). When we move out of legalism, we're free from condemnation, free to love and free to be led by the Holy Spirit. We must cultivate a sensitivity to the Holy Spirit so He can change our self-centered efforts into a life that produces love—a life that is led by the Spirit.

Eleven

DELIVERANCE FROM THE WORLD

S*UCCESS.* IT'S A GOAL PURSUED BY MANY, obtained by few. In our society, we have interpreted the word to mean financial prosperity and riches. Even in the Christian community we interpret it to mean extravagant churches buildings, television ministries, and influence. The Bible talks about success and prosperity, but it may not look like what we in the Western church think it should be.

Do you know what is the greatest success story in history? It has nothing to do with the advent of the wheel or the invention of the computer. The greatest success story in human history was the crucifixion of Jesus on the cross. The crucifixion—a sign of success?

What is success and prosperity? It is fulfilling God's purposes for your life. For Jesus, it was dying on the cross. Was He victorious? By the standards of the world, He was a total defeat. By God's standards, He was totally victorious. He defeated the principalities and powers of hell through His death on the cross and His resurrection from the dead.

The evidence of the work of the cross in the life of the believer is true success. The second benefit of the cross is deliverance from the world and this present age.

DELIVERANCE FROM THE WORLD ORDER

THE GREEK NEW TESTAMENT USES THREE different words for *world*. The first word, *oikoumene,* means "inhabited earth." When Caesar Augustus called a census throughout the earth, all the *oikoumene* of the Roman Empire were required to be counted in their hometown (Luke 2:1).

The second word, *kosmos* (or *cosmos*) means "order, arrangement or adornment." It doesn't refer to the physical earth but rather an ordered belief or system. It's a figure of speech meaning a realm where certain things operate in a certain way. On the night He was betrayed, Jesus prayed for His disciples, "My prayer is not that you take them out of the world but that you *protect them from the evil one"* (John 17:15, NIV, italics added). Jesus was praying that His disciples would escape the influence of the evil one—Satan—and his ordered system of beliefs that operate in rebellion against God.

By the nature of its starting point, this world's system is unable to submit to God's righteous government because it begins apart from God. When we come to the cross, we're released from this world's system and its attitudes. People who are born of God are not of this world's system. When we are totally submitted to the rule of God in our life, we cannot be under its dominion.

Deliverance From the World

We're released from the world's opinions, values, judgments, pressures, enticements, and deceptions. Our present world system is controlled by Satan, "the whole world"—*cosmos*—"is under the control of the evil one" (1 John 5:19, NIV). Once Christians come under the influence of the world, they come under deception.

The Spirit of God and the spirit of this world are diametrically opposed to one another. Paul writes in 1 Corinthians 2:12, "Now we have received, not the spirit of the world, but the spirit which is of God; that we might know the things that are freely given to us of God." The spirit of this world, Satan, obscures the work of the cross and all the things freely given to us by God. The spirit of the world *obscures,* the Spirit of God *reveals* to us the free work of the cross.

If you are in Christ, you cannot participate in a world order that is contrary to Scripture because the two are in conflict. Through the cross, Jesus has delivered you out of the power of that world system into a different order. The church is called an *ekklesia,* which means "the called out ones." As Christians, we're called out from the world system which operates under the rule of Satan and called into the order of the kingdom of God.

Have you ever stopped to think that it is God's intention to deliver you out of this present evil age? The vast majority of Christians wrongly assume that this means the Rapture. I believe that Jesus will someday come back, but that is not what He's talking about here. There is an escape from this present evil world system through the cross. Not escaping the physical earth but being delivered from its corrupting influence and alluring enticements. Through the cross you can be in the world and not of it.

The Results of Deliverance From the World's System

When we refuse to accede to the world's system, we open ourselves up to the life-transforming work of the Holy Spirit in our lives. God changes us from the inside. The first result of being delivered from the world is an intrinsic commitment to Christ's kingdom. Jesus said, "But seek first his kingdom and his righteousness, and all these things will be given to you as well. Therefore do not worry about tomorrow, for tomorrow will worry about itself. Each day has enough trouble of its own" (Matt. 6:33–34, NIV).

In my life, I have found that every time I've sought Him and His righteousness, everything else has been added to me. When I go after everything else in the world and put Him in the back seat, it never works out right. Never. Trying to keep up with the Joneses is not important. What's important is living a life of success in the eyes of our heavenly Father. What's important is looking for God's approval, not the world's. There is a freedom that comes from letting the cares of this world go and letting God worry about tomorrow.

When I'm free from the world's system, I'm free from Satan's manipulation and deception. When we seek first the kingdom of God, we see through the world's schemes. The media tell us, "You only go around once in life, baby, get all the gusto you can." When we seek the kingdom first, we see that statements such as "going for the gusto" are really rooted in selfishness and indulgence.

The world system, and our society, is hooked, driven, and controlled by selfishness. But God says through the cross we're set free from the influences of this world. We're set free from self. We're set free from the dominion of sin. It has no more manipulation of what we think and feel.

When we're free from the influence of this world's system, we have the strength to refuse to bow down before the world's idols. And what are the world's idols? Success, popularity, wealth, power, pleasure, and comfort. When we live with an eternal perspective, what matters most is what God thinks, not what our neighbor thinks. What's most important is living by God's definition of success—which begins at the cross.

DELIVERANCE FROM THIS PRESENT AGE

THE THIRD GREEK WORD FOR WORLD is *eon* (or *aeon*), and it refers to "an age or measure of time." The Word of God tells us that this present age is evil, but on the cross, Jesus delivered us from it.

> Grace and peace to you from God our Father and the Lord Jesus Christ, who gave himself for our sins to rescue us from the present evil age, according to the will of our God and Father.
> —Galatians 1:3–4, NIV

Paul describes Jesus as the One "who gave himself for our sins to rescue us from the present evil age." Jesus died on the cross that we might be delivered from this present age. When you realize God has delivered you from this present age, you place yourself in a position where He can work in you and through you.

God's Word can help us to understand this present age—and its future.

THE PRESENT EVIL AGE IS COMING TO A CONCLUSION

IN THE PARABLE OF THE SOWER and the seed, Jesus describes the fate of the one who sows the tares among the wheat:

The enemy who sows them is the devil. The harvest is the *end of the age,* and the harvesters are angels.

As the weeds are pulled up and burned in the fire, so it will be at the *end of the age.* The Son of Man will send out his angels, and they will weed out of his kingdom everything that causes sin and all who do evil. They will throw them into the fiery furnace, where there will be weeping and gnashing of teeth. Then the righteous will shine like the sun in the kingdom of their Father. He who has ears, let him hear.

—Matthew 13:37–43, NIV, italics added

According to Jesus' parable, this present age is not going to continue forever. God warned us that this present evil age is coming to a conclusion. However the good and evil will exist together until then. in fact, He says, don't even try to callout the tares since you might get some wheat in the process. That's why the Father does it at the end of the age. They're growing together in the same field—in the church—the wheat and tares, wicked and just, flesh and Spirit. They may look religious—witchcraft always appears that way—but they are still wicked. Jesus says that at the end of the age, the wicked will be gathered first to be burned.

SATAN IS THE GOD OF THIS PRESENT AGE

SATAN IS CALLED THE GOD OF this present age. "And even if our gospel is veiled, it is veiled to those who are perishing. The god of this age has blinded the minds of unbelievers, so that they cannot see the light of the gospel of the glory of Christ, who is the image of God" (2 Cor. 4:3–4, NIV). Any person who has been exposed to the claims of Jesus Christ but refuses to give his life to

Him has been blinded by the god of this present world system—Satan.

Satan tries to delay the end of this present age because when it ends he will be cast into the lake of fire and brimstone to be burned and tormented day and night forever (Rev. 20:10). If you knew that in the age to come, you were going to be cast into the lake of fire, you would do whatever you could to prevent its coming. Because it's the church that ushers in the end of the age, he's fighting us. Jesus said the end of the age—the *aeon*—wouldn't occur until the gospel is preached to the inhabitants—the *oikoumene*—of the whole world (Matt. 24:14). Satan is battling the church in order to delay his eventual demise.

As we rise up and take the victory Jesus won against the devil, we usher in the coming of Christ's kingdom. That's why Satan tries so hard to corrupt the church and its people. His use of Jezebels and Lucifers is simply a stall tactic. He infuses churches with legalism so that the word of our testimony is rendered powerless to ourselves and the unsaved. He barrages us with guilt and condemnation so that we have no confidence in our testimony. Nominal, powerless Christians have no power over Satan and act as his accessories in stalling the end of the age. Most of all, he obscures the work of the cross because he knows it is in the cross that his defeat is quickened. The more effective Satan is in keeping the church from fulfilling its purpose in God, the more time he has before judgment.

WE'VE ALREADY TASTED OF THE POWER OF THE AGE TO COME

It is impossible for those who have once been enlightened, who have tasted the heavenly gift, who have shared in the Holy Spirit, who have

133

tasted the goodness of the word of God and the powers of the coming age, if they fall away, to be brought back to repentance.

—Hebrews 6:4–6, NIV

There is a correlation between sharing in the Holy Spirit and tasting in the goodness of the Word of God and the powers of the coming age. I believe God has given us a little taste of the age to come to spoil our taste for this present age. When we share in the Holy Spirit we actually become the Spirit's partner in ministry. We can choose to be Satan's accessory in stalling the end of the age, or we can partner with the Holy Spirit in ministry and in ushering in the age to come. The infilling of the Holy Spirit enables us to taste of the Word of God and of what the power of the next age will be like.

John Wimber once told me, "If you ever pray for a sick person and they get well, if you ever pray for a demonized person and they go free, if you ever pray for somebody to be filled with the Holy Spirit and you see the power of God, you'll never stop; you'll be hooked for the rest of your life." You can't partner with the Holy Spirit in healing, delivering, or leading someone to Christ without getting hooked because once you've tasted of the age to come, you never want to go back.

How does tasting of the age to come affect you? It makes you hungry for more, and it draws you away from this present age. You aren't delivered from this present age by saying, "This present age is bad; I won't lust; I won't cheat; I won't overeat." That's focusing on the negative rather than the positive. You have to substitute it with something else. Get a taste of the Spirit of God and the age to come, and you'll lose your taste for the present age.

Deliverance From the World

THE CARES OF THIS WORLD MAKE US UNFRUITFUL

IN THE SAME PARABLE OF THE SOWER that we studied before, Jesus talked about the seed sown among the thorns: "What was sown among the thorns is the man who hears the word, but the worries of this life and the deceitfulness of wealth choke it, making it unfruitful" (Matt. 13:22, NIV). The word for *wealth* is the same word, *aeon,* that is translated "world or age." The present age is deceitful and will choke the effect of the Word of God in your life, making you unfruitful. If you allow this present age to become your focus, you'll be more concerned about becoming a success in the eyes of the world rather than a success in the eyes of God. Remember, Jesus' greatest success occurred while He hung on a cross.

CHANGE BEGINS FIRST IN THE MIND

"AND BE NOT CONFORMED TO THIS WORLD: but be ye transformed by the renewing of your mind, that ye may prove what is that good, and acceptable, and perfect, will of God" (Rom. 12:2). *World* here, again, is the word *aeon.* Do not be conformed to this present *age,* but be transformed by the renewing of your mind. Spiritual change doesn't take place by adding more religious rules, it begins in the mind. "For as he thinketh in his heart, so is he" (Prov. 23:7). When you think different, you live different. Change begins in the mind.

It's the Holy Spirit who changes my thinking, my ambition, my goals, my priorities; then I begin to live different. The carnal, unrenewed mind is the enemy of God. No one shares their secrets with their enemy, and neither does God. But if your mind is renewed, God will share with you His secrets. He'll reveal His plan for your life. Those who conform to this present age will never discover God's good, perfect, and acceptable will for their lives.

One of the great tragedies of the New Testament concerned a gifted young man named Demas. Paul says, "For Demas hath forsaken me, having loved this present world" (2 Tim. 4:10). It doesn't say Demas got drunk; it doesn't say Demas stole some money; it doesn't say Demas had an immoral affair. What does it say? He loved this present age. He immersed himself in it and could no longer walk with Paul because Paul wasn't walking according to this present age. Here was a man who was being mentored by the greatest missionary in the history of the church. He saw people being saved, healed, and delivered. But Demas became enamored with the present age and couldn't go on. The tragic part of Demas' story is this: *he sacrificed God's destiny for the present age.*

The Benefits of Deliverance From This Age

Join with others in following my example, brothers, and take note of those who live according to the pattern we gave you. For, as I have often told you before and now say again even with tears, many live as enemies of the cross of Christ. Their destiny is destruction, their god is their stomach, and their glory is in their shame. Their mind is on earthly things. But our citizenship is in heaven. And we eagerly await a Savior from there, the Lord Jesus Christ, who, by the power that enables him to bring everything under his control, will transform our lowly bodies so that they will be like his glorious body.

—Philippians 3:17–21, NIV

When we refuse to be enticed by the allure of this present age, God rewards us with two benefits.

First, we get a vision of our citizenship in heaven. In this passage, Paul isn't talking about unbelievers; he's talking about Christians in the church. Why would he rebuke a lost, unregenerate person under the influence of this present age? He says many live as enemies of the cross. The people are walking with God, they're Christians, yet they are enemies—not of Jesus, but of the cross. Doesn't witchcraft obscure the cross of Jesus? The enemies of the cross have settled for what the present age has offered them and have made indulgence and earthly things their god. Paul reminds them, however, that their citizenship is in heaven.

Citizenship has its rights and privileges. As a citizen, you are given free access to enter and exit your respective country. As citizens of heaven, you have the right to enter and exit the presence of God. Even in a foreign land, the citizen is granted the special privileges and immunities due to the nation of which they are a citizen. In New Testament times, a Roman citizen could not be punished without a trial. No other citizen had the rights and privileges of the Romans. No other citizen has the rights and privileges of the citizens of heaven. As a citizen of the United States, I hold two citizenships. But the only one that is important to me is the heavenly citizenship, and that comes by accepting what Jesus did for me at Calvary.

A second benefit of being delivered from this present age is that we live with the expectation of Christ's return. Paul writes, "And we eagerly await a Savior from there, the Lord Jesus Christ, who, by the power that enables him to bring everything under his control, will transform our lowly bodies so that they will be like his glorious body" (Phil. 3:20–21).

If you haven't been delivered from this present evil

age, you're not looking with excitement to the Lord's return. As a child, did your parents ever leave you alone at home, admonishing you to take care of things, and then return when you least expected them? Because you hadn't taken care of the things they told you to do, you knew that what was coming next would not be happy.

Once while growing up I broke a very expensive piece of furniture while my parents were away. I was not eagerly, earnestly looking for my parents' return. In fact, I dreaded their return. It brought horror and fear to my heart because I knew it was going to bring horror and pain to my backside when my daddy got home. And it did.

As believers we don't have to live in fear of eventual punishment when we get to heaven, but as citizens of heaven, we live with an eager expectation of the return of Jesus.

If we don't live in anticipation of our Lord's return, chances are there is something about this present age that has a hold on us. If we dread the Lord's return, there obviously is an issue that needs to be death with and brought under the blood.

Praise God, if you find you are enticed by the allure of this present age, the blood of Jesus is sufficient to free you. It is for freedom that Christ has set us free, and it is for freedom that we are freed from the enticements of this world system and present age.

Twelve

DELIVERANCE FROM OURSELVES

THE GREATEST BATTLE EVERY PERSON FIGHTS is the battle within. Pogo, the cartoon character, rightly identified our common, primary adversary, "We have met the enemy, and he is us." Our greatest need is deliverance from ourselves.

Every person makes choices which determine the course of his life. As far back as Moses, people have been given two choices: life or death (see Deut. 30:11–20). When we choose death—knowingly or unknowingly—we open ourselves up to an attack from the evil one. Should we choose life, God takes us on a road that begins with salvation, runs through the cross, and ends in eternity with the Father.

Paul articulates well his struggle with his greatest enemy:

> For in my inner being I delight in God's law; but I see another law at work in the members of my body, waging war against the law of my mind and making me a prisoner of the law of sin at work within my members. What a wretched man I am! Who will rescue me from this body of death? Thanks be to God—through Jesus Christ our Lord!
> —Romans 7:22–25

Paul's greatest struggle was not against Satan, it was against himself. His flesh gave him more fits than Satan! When we live by the flesh, we partner with Satan and counteract God's plan for our lives. Sin doesn't reside in our physical bodies—it resides in our sinful nature resident within our person. Who can deliver us from our own sinful nature? Thanks be to God, we have a way out, and it is through the cross of Christ!

The word *flesh* takes on a wide range of definitions in the New Testament including "the physical body." But when Paul uses it in this context, he is referring to the old Adamic, unregenerate, rebellious, carnal nature. He literally calls it "the old man." When we come to Christ, God creates us into new people. "Therefore, if anyone is in Christ, he is a new creation; the old has gone, the new has come!" (2 Cor. 5:17, NIV). But before that new creation, we remain the old or former man. The flesh, then, is that place within that influences us to sin.

TWO TENDENCIES, A COMMON STRUGGLE

ANY MOTIVATION THAT CENTERS on feeding or promoting one's self is from the flesh. For the most part, people respond to one of two self-motivators. The first motivator is an unhealthy self-image. People with an unhealthy self-image tell themselves, "I'm nothing; I'm a nobody; I'll never amount to anything." Such self-deprecating feelings are not the result of an inferiority complex—they arise out of a self complex. One focuses on self, not on Christ. There's no virtue in that. Without Christ we can do nothing, but with Christ, we can do anything. Paul said "I can everything *through him* who gives me strength" (Phil. 4:13, italics added, NIV).

The second is overbearing pride. People who struggle with pride wrongly believe, "*I* can do all things"—not necessarily *through Christ*. Interestingly enough, the focus once again is on self, not on Christ. There's no virtue in that either. The power of God is made perfect in our weakness—not in our strength. It's when we are weak that the power of God is strong (2 Cor. 12:9–10). Both motivations, like conceit and inferiority, arise from an uncrucified self.

KEY TO THE BATTLE: CONTROL OF THE SELF

THE KEY TO DEALING WITH THE FLESH LIES in the battle for control of the self. The self is that part of us that decides whether or not to accede to our fleshly, sinful desires. Self has an insatiable appetite and has two telltale identifying phrases: *I want* and *give me*. It says, "I want the nicest car." "I want the most money." "Give me the best seat." "Give me the biggest piece of pie." *Self* is fond of talking about its two favorite people—*I* and *me*. Believers who do so haven't learned to bring their selves to the cross.

What's the solution? Paul says, "Do nothing out of selfish ambition or vain conceit, but in humility consider others better than yourselves" (Phil. 2:3, NIV). First of all, be mindful of what motivates you to action. Paul says to do *nothing* out of selfish ambition or conceit. If we are doing the right things for the wrong reasons, we need to stop. Either our motivation needs to change, or if possible, we need to step away from the responsibilities that draw attention to ourselves until we can fulfill those responsibilities for the right reasons. That can be done only after the self has been crucified. If we operate in humility we will not operate in selfish ambition or conceit.

The good news for every person is that through the cross of Jesus we are delivered from self. Paul writes in Galatians 2:20: "I am crucified with Christ: nevertheless I live; yet not I, but Christ liveth in me: and the life which I now live in the flesh I live by the faith of the Son of God, who loved me, and gave himself for me." Paul crucified his "I"—his self. You cannot find the fullness of God's will until you allow the cross to put your "I" and "me" to death.

A DECISION AND A CONFESSION

TWO THINGS MUST HAPPEN IN MY LIFE before my "I" can be crucified with Christ. *I* must make a decision, and *I* must make a confession. I must first make a cognizant, intentional decision to die to self. The death of self doesn't happen on its own. If I let self go, it will naturally gravitate to selfish motivations. Second, I must make a personal confession. Paul makes his confession his personal testimony, "I am crucified with Christ." As we confess our own crucifixion, it becomes a part of us.

Then we live it. It's one thing to talk about the death of self in general terms, but it's another thing to apply it personally. Paul says, "Now those who belong to Christ Jesus have crucified the flesh with its passions and desires" (Gal. 5:24, NAS). We may be delivered from control of the flesh, but the responsibility of crucifying it still lies with us. Dying to self means refusing to pursue our passions and desires.

Deliverance From Ourselves

REMEDY FOR THE FLESH—EXECUTION

IT IS INTERESTING TO NOTE THAT EVEN THOUGH he was a new creation, Paul still battled with his flesh. In His divine wisdom, God creates us anew after we come to Christ, but He doesn't remove our sinful nature.

Although not exhaustive, Paul gives a running list of the deeds of the flesh: sexual immorality, impurity and debauchery, idolatry and witchcraft, hatred, discord, jealousy, fits of rage, selfish ambition, dissensions, factions and envy, drunkenness, orgies, and the like. He goes on to describe the fruit of such behavior: "I warn you, as I did before, that those who live like this will not inherit the kingdom of God" (Gal. 5:21, NIV).

What is God's remedy for the flesh? "Now those who belong to Christ Jesus have crucified the flesh with its passions and desires" (Gal. 5:24, NAS). We don't send our old man to Sunday school; we don't reform him; we don't give him counseling; we don't get him to memorize Scripture. *We kill him.* Execution is the only remedy for my old man. In fact, our evidence for belonging to Christ is the crucifixion of our flesh. As we die to our self, our flesh begins to decrease, and the Spirit of God within us begins to increase.

The flesh and the Spirit are enemies—they work in opposition to one another. "For the flesh lusteth sets its desire against the Spirit, and the Spirit against the flesh; *these are in opposition to one another,* so that you may not do the things that you please" (Gal. 5:17, NAS, italics added). Our fleshly nature, that is before God changes it, is in total opposition to the Spirit of God. When we are controlled by the flesh—our sins and desires—we cannot live a life that is pleasing to God. "So then they that are in the flesh *cannot* please God" (Rom. 8:8, italics added).

Even when we do the right things for wrong,

143

selfish-motivated reasons, we still cannot please God. Jesus denounced the Pharisees for praying and tithing (Matt. 23:13). Why? They tithed for the wrong reasons— their prayers and gifts were given to draw attention to themselves.

If we want to live in Christ, the responsibility of putting to death the deeds of the flesh belongs to us. Paul says, "But if ye through the Spirit do mortify the deeds of the body, ye shall live" (Rom. 8:13). Christ has made it possible for us to die to ourselves, but the responsibility still lies with us.

Short-Term Pain for a Long-Term Gain

The cross involves pain and suffering. It's the most painful way to die that man could devise, but it's much better than the alternative.

Gloria met Dan while she was attending college. Before they met, Dan had been pretty wild, but since they began spending time together, he was calming down. As their relationship deepened, Dan started going to church with Gloria. When asked about his faith, he replied, "I love God, and I think going to church is very important. But it's so personal that I don't feel comfortable talking about it."

One day he proposed to Gloria. She excitedly rushed to share the good news with her family, but she was ill-prepared for their lack of enthusiasm. The family sat down with her and explained their reservations regarding Dan. They sensed something just wasn't right.

A few days later, the family met with Gloria and their pastor to discuss their concerns further. "Gloria," the pastor began, "what concerns us is Dan's walk with the Lord. We're not so sure that his transformation is real. He never shares with others what God is doing in his life. Our discernment leads us to believe that he doesn't really care at all about Christ. He's going to church for you, not for himself. Once you get married, we're concerned he will only revert back to the old Dan. You're totally committed to Christ and His righteousness, but by marrying Dan, you'll be unequally yoked. Our advice is to break off your relationship with him."

At the end of the meeting, Gloria said she would pray about it. After much prayer, Gloria decided to break off her engagement with Dan.

Was that painful for Gloria? You bet it was. It was just like getting shot. When there is an emotional attachment, two spirits are united creating a soul tie. That's why it's painful at first to pull away, but God gives the strength to endure to victory.

What if Gloria had married Dan, and he turned out to be the person her family warned her about? After a year, Dan would suddenly lose interest in God and the church, eventually going back to his old lifestyle. What used to be a cheerful, energetic young woman would turn into a discouraged, uninvolved, church attendee. People would recognize the change in Gloria since her marriage to Dan. Three children and thirteen years later, he would divorce her, leaving her for another woman. She would be left to raise the children alone. Her pain would go on and on, entering the lives of her children, and continue into their lives and marriages.

There is a *right* kind of pain and there is a *wrong* kind of pain. The pain Gloria would endure in the imagined scenario above is the wrong kind of pain. If she had taken the pain of the cross, saying, "Self, you won't do it. You will die. You will go ahead and hurt, but God is in control!", she would have found the fruit of life and righteousness. *Dying to self often means short-term pain for long-term gain.*

You will have long-term pain by choosing unrighteousness. You may like to get ahead: make a little more money; take a few shortcuts. But unless self goes to the cross and suffers the pain of crucifixion, the pain self reaps down the road will be three times greater. There is a short-term cost to picking up your cross, and there is a greater long-term cost in not picking it up.

Even Spiritual Things Can Be Rooted in Self

THE IRONY IS, WE CAN DO SOME VERY spiritual things that are rooted in self. We can invest all of our time in church leadership at the expense of our families, never spending time with them. *Self wanted to feel important.* We can sing in church and participate on the worship team but falter when we come under the attack of the enemy. *Self wanted to be in front of people.* People that fall under the control of a Jezebel or Lucifer spirit are people who failed to bring their personal hurt to the cross. *Self then stepped in to operate under a guise of spirituality.*

Jesus said, "What good is it for a man to gain the whole world, and yet lose or forfeit his very self?" (Luke 9:25, NIV). We can gain prestige and power—even in the Christian world—and yet, in the end, damage or destroy our lives. Jesus prefaced His question with a clarion call, "If anyone would come after me, he must deny himself and take up his cross daily and follow me" (Luke 9:23, NIV). You cannot follow Jesus until you deny yourself. Self doesn't want to go where Jesus is going. Self wants to avoid the pain of crucifixion.

The Cross: The Intersection of God's Will and My Will

DENYING MYSELF MEANS SAYING *no* to what I want, to what I feel, to what I think I deserve. The act of taking up one's cross has been defined as reaching the place

146

where my will and God's will intersect and choosing God's will over my own. Every person reaches this point at some time in his life. Jesus' will crossed with God's will in the Garden of Gethsemane. The night of His betrayal, Jesus prayed, "Father, if you are willing, take this cup from me; yet not my will, but yours be done" (Luke 22:42, NIV). Jesus could have backed out of the cross and said, "Let man go to hell. I don't want to do it." He did not have to die for us. He could have stayed in heaven. He could have said, "I don't need this." But He did it out of His submission to the Father.

The point of intersection between God's will and our will means different things to different people. Some people play with lustful thoughts. Others may cheat on their taxes or find it difficult to admit when they are wrong. Still others always work their way to the front of the line when their church has a potluck. It would be impossible to list all the ways that self rears its ugly head, but suffice it to say, dying to self boils down to a willingness to prefer others above ourselves.

In the middle ages, certain ascetics interpreted dying to themselves to mean they had to make their lives as uncomfortable as possible in hopes that it would mortify their flesh. As a result, some ascetics wore shirts of hair or slept on beds of nails. Those people confused their physical flesh with their soulish flesh. Mortifying their flesh became such a consuming passion that it became as idol worship in that they were consumed by the act. The physical body in itself isn't sinful. When God created it, He called it good. The problem isn't with the physical body; it's with the sinful nature.

THE RESULTS OF DELIVERANCE FROM OURSELVES

AS BENEFICIARIES OF CHRIST'S REDEMPTION, WE ARE GRANTED several benefits of deliverance from sin.

Freedom from the dominion of sin

The first benefit of deliverance from ourselves is freedom from the dominion of sin. "For sin shall not have dominion over you: for ye are not under the law, but under grace" (Rom. 6:14). When we come to Jesus, the power that causes us to sin gives way to the power to resist sin. Because we are born in sin, before we came to Christ, we could not prevent sinning. However, because of Jesus' work on the cross, we have the power to overcome sin. We no longer have to sin. We're free to serve God. We're free to live a life of righteousness—a life that is pleasing to our heavenly Father. A life where the Father speaks to us, "Well done, My good and faithful servant."

People look at the lives of some Christians and say, "I don't want to be a Christian because then I won't be able to do what *I* want." That's self talking. Because of Christ, we can respond, "Because I'm a Christian, I don't have to do what my desires tell me to do."

Dogs, like all animals, go wherever their desires lead them. If they want to eat trash and drink out of a toilet, they do it. We shake our heads and laugh at them. It works, however, the same way with us. When we are led by our passions and desires, invariably, we settle on consuming things that are ultimately harmful to our spirits. We eat spiritual trash and drink out of spiritual toilets! And God just shakes His head; but He isn't laughing—He's grieved. When we have been set free from the dominion of sin, we see our life from God's perspective. Only then will we no longer settle for anything less than His best for our lives and our best for Him.

Deliverance From Ourselves

Freedom to serve

The second benefit of being delivered from ourselves is the freedom to serve.

> Jesus called them together and said, "You know that those who are regarded as rulers of the Gentiles lord it over them, and their high officials exercise authority over them. Not so with you. Instead, whoever wants to become great among you must be your servant, and whoever wants to be first must be slave of all. For even the Son of Man did not come to be served, but to serve, and to give his life as a ransom for many."
> —Mark 10:42–45, NIV

The path to authority and leadership in the church lies in servanthood. Jesus—God clothed in human flesh—entered our world the first time not to be served but to serve. The carnal mind would assume that if God were to come down to earth, He would take control by force. But anybody who comes to power without serving will not be able to use their authority correctly because they haven't learned to die to self.

If you want a promotion in the kingdom, the way up is down. But that's not so in this present evil age. The world tells us, "Get there first; get the most." "He who dies with the most toys wins." We are told by some that financial independence is the goal—that way we won't have to work for anyone else. Such a statement really says, "*We* won't have to *serve* anyone else." In the kingdom of God, it's the opposite. If you want to live, you die. If you want to get, you give. If you want to go up, you go down. It's the rule by which the kingdom of God operates. Unfortunately, so few want to serve and so many want to be served. This is the essence of pride.

My grandfather used to say that there are only two businesses where you can start at the top—grave digging and well digging. Everywhere else you start at the bottom. And that's true in the kingdom of God—you start at the bottom. If people are given authority and visibility too early, they'll abuse it. Always. And that applies anywhere in church leadership. Let a man first be proven. And then bring him into leadership.

When we have been delivered from ourselves, we find freedom in serving. When we haven't died to self, we confuse God's design for our promotion with our own design.

Freedom from self-promotion

The third benefit of deliverance from ourselves is the freedom from self-promotion.

"For we preach not ourselves, but Christ Jesus the Lord; and ourselves your servants for Jesus' sake" (2 Cor. 4:5). Wherever Paul went, he preached Christ. He could have built a big name for himself, but he didn't. With such a successful ministry, Paul could have developed his own set of followers, but he didn't. He didn't preach himself, he preached Christ.

When we walk in freedom from self-promotion, we give God ample opportunity to promote us in His time. When we promote ourselves, we wrest the control of God's blessing from Him and ultimately, from ourselves.

Freedom from proving yourself right

The fourth benefit of deliverance from ourselves is the freedom from the need to prove ourselves right. When you die to your self, you don't always have to be right. Defensiveness on the part of a believer is evidence of an uncrucified self. But by executing the flesh, we open ourselves to hearing from God—however He may choose to speak to us.

Have you ever noticed that although everybody will admit that no one is perfect, few are willing to admit that *they* are not? By becoming defensive with our weaknesses, we cut ourselves off from God's means of molding us and forming us into the men and women God wants us to be.

When a person gives us a word we believe to be from God during a church service, are we willing to have that word tested by the body and by church leadership? If not, then there is evidence that we have not died to ourselves. No person is above question. There is nothing more empowering to a congregation than when a person stands up and humbly acknowledges that the word they gave wasn't 100 percent right on. Rather than thwarting the gifts, such humility gives people the confidence to move out, knowing they can do so in a safe, authentic environment.

It's a great mockery of the church when believers fight one another, trying to prove each other wrong. Often the doctrine of the two sides is not the issue— each side is trying to save face. We shouldn't be fighting about the Rapture, or the Millennium, or dozens of other points of conflict within the body. The only thing we should be fighting for is a glorious church. We'll find out soon enough who missed the Rapture. The only thing worth fighting for is that we are a glorious church prepared for our bridegroom, Jesus Christ—and our enemy is not another believer, our enemy is Satan.

Conclusion

CROSSING THE BRIDGE

MANY PEOPLE ARE STANDING on this side of heaven, looking across to the other side. They desire the full purposes of God for their lives but believe that in order to use the bridge that stretches from one side to the other—which is Christ—they must pay a toll. As they approach the bridge, they see the toll booth and assume that either they don't have enough money, or the currency they carry isn't acceptable to the toll booth attendant. Sadly enough, people assume they must have the right job experience or know the right people in order to pass. There is only one person you need to know—Jesus Christ.

If you have given your life to Jesus Christ, you can walk up to the toll booth where the worker will tell you to cross because your toll is paid. The toll has already been paid because of the cross of Jesus Christ. Jesus not only gave us great blessings through the cross but He wants the cross to work in us. Jesus' physical body was taken to heaven via the cross. His spiritual body, the church, will also be taken to heaven via the cross.

For some believers, the cross has certainly worked *for* them, but it's done very little *in* them. What about you—have you applied the cross *to* your life? Is the cross working *in* your life?

I didn't ask if you are saved. I asked, "Has the cross done its work *in* you?" You're delivered from the law, from the world, from yourself—those are your benefits—but are you still living outside the work of the cross?

It's only as the cross completes its work within our lives that we can be released from the influence of witchcraft. The cross breaks the power of manipulation, domination, intimidation, control, legalism, and condemnation.

The underlying theme in this book is freedom. Witchcraft, like any other bondage, operates in control. Paul wrote in Galatians 5:1, "It is for freedom that Christ has set us free. Stand firm, then, and do not let yourselves be burdened again by a yoke of slavery" (NIV). Christ has already set us free. We're free!

Do not allow yourself to be burdened again by a yoke of slavery to witchcraft. Let this verse serve as your own emancipation proclamation. You're free!

Because of Christ's work on the cross, we're set free from the dominion of sin in our lives. But like a dog who doesn't know his leash has been unchained, we may remain in familiar territory, lacking the confidence to venture out into the uncharted territory of God's glorious grace.

Break that chain. Untie that leash. Step out in the

freedom the cross of Christ has won for you. It's not a matter of following a set of principles in some book—including this one. It's a matter of being led by the Holy Spirit. Allow the Holy Spirit to lead you. Use the Word of God as your guide. God wants to take you into new realms of uncharted territory. If Christ has set you free, you are free indeed (John 8:36).

May God richly bless you as walk in the power of the cross.

Appendix

DEALING WITH THE ROOTS OF DEMONIC STRONGHOLDS

THE OBJECTIVE of this appendix is to teach believers how to recognize the fruit of a particular demonic stronghold, locate the root of the stronghold through the scriptural reference, and loose the power of the Holy Spirit to complete the deliverance.

> For though we live in the world, we do not wage war as the world does. The weapons we fight with are not the weapons of the world. On the contrary, they have divine power to *demolish* strongholds.
> —2 Corinthians 10:3–4, NIV, italics added

LEGEND:

Spirit   Sixteen demonic strongholds
Fruit   The fruit of those demonic strongholds
Scriptures   Scriptural references which describe the fruit of the demonic strongholds
Loose   Scriptures that loose the power of the Holy Spirit

SPIRIT	FRUIT	SUGGESTED SCRIPTURES	LOOSE
HAUGHTINESS	Pride	Proverbs 6:16–17 Proverbs 16:18–19 Proverbs 28:25 Isaiah 16:6	**A humble and contrite spirit** **Proverbs 16:19** **Romans 1:4**
	Idleness	Ezekiel 16:48, 50	
	Arrogance, Smugness	2 Samuel 22:28 Jeremiah 48:29 Isaiah 2:11, 17; 5:15	
	Obstinance	Proverbs 29:1 Daniel 5:30	
	Rebellion	1 Samuel 15:23 Proverbs 29:1	
	Scorn	Proverbs 1:22; 3:34 Proverbs 21:24; 29:8	
	Strife	Proverbs 28:25	
	Contentiousness	Proverbs 13:10	
	Rejection (of God)	Psalm 10:4 Jeremiah 43:2	
	Self-Deception	Jeremiah 49:16 Obadiah 1:3	
	Self-Righteousness	Luke 18:11–12	
HEAVINESS	Excessive Mourning Rejection	Luke 4:18	**Comforter, Oil of Joy, Garment of Praise**
	Insomnia	Nehemiah 2:2	**John 15:26** **Isaiah 61:3**
	Self-Pity	Psalm 69:20	
	Sorrow, Grief	Nehemiah 2:2 Proverbs 15:13	

158

Appendix

SPIRIT	FRUIT	SUGGESTED SCRIPTURES	LOOSE
HEAVINESS, continued	Brokenhearted	Psalm 69:20; Luke 4:18 Proverbs 12:18; 18:14; 15:3, 13	**Comforter, Oil of Joy, Garment of Praise**
	Despair, Dejection, Hopelessness	2 Corinthians 1:8–9	**John 15:26 Isaiah 61:3**
	Inner Hurts, Torn Spirit	Luke 4:18 Proverbs 18:14; 26:22	
	Heaviness, Depression	Isaiah 61:3	
	Suicide	Mark 9	
JEALOUSY	Murder	Genesis 4:8	**Love of God**
	Hate	Genesis 37:3–4, 8 1 Thessalonians 4:8	**1 Corinthians 13 Ephesians 5:2**
	Anger, Rage	Genesis 4:5–6 Proverbs 6:34; 14:29, 22:24–25; 29:22–23	
	Revenge, Spite	Proverbs 6:34; 14:16–17	
	Cruelty	Song of Solomon 8:6 Proverbs 27:4	
	Jealousy	Numbers 5:14 Song of Solomon 8:6	
	Dissension	Galatians 5:19	
	Competition	Genesis 4:4–5	
	Strife	Proverbs 10:12	
	Envy	Proverbs 14:30	
	Contention	Proverbs 13:10	

SPIRIT	FRUIT	SUGGESTED SCRIPTURES	LOOSE
LYING SPIRIT	Strong Deceptions	2 Thessalonians 2:9–13	**Spirit of Truth**
	Superstitions	1 Timothy 4:7	**John 14:17; 15:26; 16:13**
	Accusations	Revelation 12:10 Psalm 31:18	
	Flattery	Psalm 78:36 Proverbs 20:19; 26:28; 29:5	
	False Prophecy	Jeremiah 23:16–17; 27:9–10; Matthew 7:15	
	Religious Bondage	Galatians 5:1	
	Slander	Proverbs 10:18	
	False Teachers	2 Peter	
	Gossip	1 Timothy 6:20 2 Timothy 2:16	
	Lies	2 Chronicles 18:22 Proverbs 6:16–19	
DIVINATION	Fortuneteller, Soothsayer	Micah 5:12 Isaiah 2:6	**Holy Spirit Gifts of the Spirit**
	Warlock, Witch, Sorcerer	Exodus 22:18	**1 Corinthians 9–12**
	Rebellion	1 Samuel 15:22	
	Hypnotist, Enchanter	Deuteronomy 18:11 Isaiah 19:3	
	Water Witching	Hosea 4:12	
	Magic	Exodus 7:11; 8:7; 9:11	

Appendix

SPIRIT	FRUIT	SUGGESTED SCRIPTURES	LOOSE
DIVINATION, continued	Drugs (Greek—*Pharmakos*)	Galatians 5:20 Revelation 9:21; 18:23; 21:8; 22:15	**Holy Spirit Gifts of the Spirit**
	Stargazer, Zodiac	Isaiah 47:13 Leviticus 19:26	**1 Corinthians 9–12**
	Horoscope		
		Jeremiah 10:2	
FAMILIAR SPIRIT	Necromancer	Deuteronomy 18:11 1 Chronicles 10:13	**Holy Spirit Gifts of the Spirit**
	Clairvoyant	1 Samuel 28:7–8	**1 Corinthians 12:9–12**
	Spiritist	1 Samuel 28	
	Medium	1 Samuel 28	
	Yoga	Jeremiah 29:8	
	Drugs, Hallucinogens	Revelation 9:21; 18:23, 21:8; 22:15 Galatians 5:20	
	Peeping & Muttering	Isaiah 8:19; 29:4; 59:3	
	False Prophecy	Isaiah 8:19; 29:4	
	Passivity, Dreamers	Jeremiah 23:16, 25, 32; 27:9–10	
PERVERSE SPIRIT	Wounded Spirit	Proverbs 15:4	**God's Spirit of grace and supplication**
	Evil Actions	Proverbs 17:20, 23	
	Foolishness	Proverbs 1:22; 19:1	**Zechariah 12:10 Hebrews 10:29**
	Atheist	Proverbs 14:2 Romans 1:30	

SPIRIT	FRUIT	SUGGESTED SCRIPTURES	LOOSE
PERVERSE SPIRIT, continued	Doctrinal Error	Isaiah 19:14 Romans 1:22–23 2 Timothy 3:7–8	**God's Spirit of grace and supplication**
	Chronic Worrier	Proverbs 19:3	**Zechariah 12:10** **Hebrews 10:29**
	Twisting the Word Contentious	Acts 13:10 2 Peter 2:14 Philippians 2:14, 16 1 Timothy 6:4–5 Titus 3:10–11	
	Filthy Mind	Proverbs 2:12; 23:33	
	Sex Perversions	Romans 1:17–32 2 Timothy 3:2	
SEDUCTION	Hypocritical Lies	1 Timothy 4:1 Proverbs 12:22	**Holy Spirit Truth**
	Seared Conscience	1 Timothy 4:1 James 1:14	**John 16:13**
	Attractions, fascinations	Mark 13:22	
	Wander from Truth	2 Timothy 3:13 Deuteronomy 13:6–8	
	Seducers, Enticers	1 Timothy 4:1 Proverbs 1:10 2 Timothy 3:13	
	Evil Fascinations	Proverbs 12:26	
	Deception	2 Timothy 3:13 Romans 7:11 1 John 2:18–26 2 Thessalonians 2:10	

162

Appendix

SPIRIT	FRUIT	SUGGESTED SCRIPTURES	LOOSE
WHOREDOMS	Chronic Dissatisfaction	Ezekiel 16:28	**Spirit of God Pure Spirit**
	Love of Money	Proverbs 15:27 1 Timothy 6:7–14	**Ephesians 3:16**
	Fornication	Hosea 4:13–19	
	Idolatry	Judges 2:17 Hosea 4:12 Ezekiel 16	
	Excessive Appetite	1 Corinthians 6:13–16 Philippians 3:19	
	Unfaithfulness, Adultery	Ezekiel 16:15, 28 Proverbs 5:1–14	
	Worldliness	James 4:4	
	Spirit, Soul, Body Prostitution	Ezekiel 16:15, 28 Proverbs 5:1–14	
INFIRMITY	Oppression	Acts 10:38	**Spirit of Life Gifts of Healing**
	Cancer	Luke 13:11 John 5:4	**1 Corinthians 12:9 Romans 8:2**
	Weakness	Luke 13:11 John 5:5	
	Lingering Disorders	Luke 13:11 John 5:5	
	Arthritis	John 5:5	
	Asthma, Hay Fever, Allergies	John 5:5	
	Impotent, Frail, Lame	Acts 3:2; 4:9 John 5:5	
	Bent Body, Spine	Luke 13:11	

SPIRIT	FRUIT	SUGGESTED SCRIPTURES	LOOSE
DEAF AND DUMB	Dumbness	Mark 9:25	**Resurrection Life**
	Tearing	Mark 9:18, 20, 26	**Healing**
	Foaming at the Mouth	Luke 9:39 Mark 9:39	**Romans 8:11 1 Corinthians 12:9**
	Mental Illness	Matthew 17:15 Mark 9:17; 5:5	
	Seizures, Epilepsy	Mark 9:18, 20, 26	
	Gnashing Teeth	Mark 9:18	
	Burns	Mark 9:22	
	Drownings	Mark 9:22	
	Suicide	Mark 9:22	
	Pining Away	Mark 9:18	
	Blindness	Matthew 12:22	
	Crying	Mark 9:26	
	Ear Problems	Mark 9:25–26	
	Prostration	Mark 9:26	
BONDAGE	Fears	Romans 8:15	**Liberty Spirit of Adoption**
	Addictions	Romans 8:15 2 Peter 2:19	**Romans 8:15**
	Bondage to Sin	2 Timothy 2:26	
	Captivity to Satan	2 Peter 2:19	
	Compulsive Sin	Proverbs 5:22 John 8:34	
	Servant to Corruption	Romans 6:16; 7:23 Luke 8:26–29 Acts 8:23 John 8:34	

Appendix

SPIRIT	FRUIT	SUGGESTED SCRIPTURES	LOOSE
FEAR	Fears, Phobias	Isaiah 13:7–8 2 Timothy 1:7	**Love, Power and a Sound Mind**
	Heart Attacks	Psalm 55:4 Luke 21:26 John 14:1, 27	**2 Timothy 1:7**
	Torment, Horror	Psalm 55:5 1 John 4:18	
	Fear of Death	Psalm 55:4 Hebrews 2:14–15	
	Anxiety, Stress	1 Peter 5:7	
	Untrusting, Doubt	Matthew 8:26 Revelation 21:8	
	Fear of Man	Proverbs 29:25	
ANTICHRIST	Denies Deity of Christ	1 John 4:3 2 John 7	**Spirit of Truth** **1 John 4:6**
	Denies Atonement	1 John 4:3	
	Against Christ and His Teaching	2 Thessalonians 2:4 1 John 4:3	
	Humanism	2 Thessalonians 2:3, 7	
	Worldly Speech and Actions	1 John 4:5	
	Teachers of Heresies	1 John 2:18–19	
	Against Christians	Revelation 13:7	
	Lawlessness	2 Thessalonians 2:3–12	
	Deceiver	2 Thessalonians 2:4 2 John 7	

SPIRIT	FRUIT	SUGGESTED SCRIPTURES	LOOSE
ERROR	Error	Proverbs 14:22 1 John 4:6 2 Peter 3:16–17	**Spirit of Truth** **1 John 4:6** **Psalm 51:10**
	Unsubmissive	Proverbs 29:1 1 John 4:6	
	False Doctrines	1 Timothy 6:20–21 2 Timothy 4:3 Titus 3:10 1 John 4:1–6	
	Unteachable	Proverbs 10:17; 12:1; 13:18; 15:10, 12, 32 2 Timothy 4:1–4 1 John 4:6	
	Servant of Corruption	2 Peter 2:19	
	Contentious	James 3:16	
	New Age Movement	2 Thessalonians 2 Peter 2:10	
	Defensive, Argumentative	Proverbs 29:1; 13:10 1 John 4:6	
DEATH	Destruction	Hebrews 2:14	**Life through the Word** **Faith in Christ, the Victor** **2 Corinthians 5:6–8** **Deuteronomy 30:19** **John 14:6** **Proverbs 10:2;** **18:21**

Notes

Chapter 2
Witchcraft in the Family

1. Nelson's Illustrated Bible Dictionary © 1986 Thomas Nelson Publishers. Taken from PC Bible Software © 1993, 1994 Biblesoft.

Chapter 3
Manipulation, Thy Name Is Jezebel

1. Mike Bickle, *Growing in the Prophetic,* (Lake Mary, FL: Creation House, 1996), 184.

Appendix
Dealing With the Roots of Demonic Strongholds

1. An unpublished work by Sunny S. Hand, (Dallas, TX), 1996.

Other Books by Rick Godwin:

Training for Reigning

IF YOU WANT TO STAY IN MEDIOCRITY and powerless ritual, *don't* read this book! You will be greatly challenged by these scriptural insights to grow into a real spiritual lifestyle, which Jesus taught for all of His disciples. Rick brings tremendous conviction, but also tremendous encouragement to be all God has called us to be.

Casey Treat, pastor
Christian Faith Center
Seattle, Washington

Training for Reigning and *Exposing Witchcraft in the Church* are being translated into other languages. For more information and availability, contact Rick Godwin Ministries.

Rick Godwin has over fifty tape albums and several videotapes. For availability, contact:

RICK GODWIN MINISTRIES
14015 San Pedro Avenue
San Antonio, Texas 78232-4337
800-675-3297
Fax: 210-402-0673
e-mail: rickgodwin@juno.com

Overseas Offices

In Africa:
RICK GODWIN MINISTRIES
P. O. Box 574
Randburg 2125 RSA
phone: 011-7923817
fax: 011-7936969

In Australia:
RICK GODWIN MINISTRIES
P. O. Box 1195
Castle Hill NSW 2154
Australia
phone: 02-9899-8666
fax: 612-9634-7633

In England/UK:
RICK GODWIN MINISTRIES
339 Finchley Road
Hampstead, London NW3 6EP
phone: 0171-794-7494
fax: 0171-435-8143

In Malaysia/Singapore:
RICK GODWIN MINISTRIES
10 Jalan SS2/67
47300 Petaling Jaya
Selangor, Malaysia
phone: 03-7745350
fax: 03-7743971

About the Author

Rick Godwin is the founder and senior pastor of Eagle's Nest Christian Fellowship in San Antonio, Texas, a non-denominational church. He also ministers extensively throughout the United States and internationally. His message strongly challenges the church to rise to new heights in Christ by stepping across the lines of apathy, tradition, cultural, and religious barriers in order to make a difference and help change our world.

"Rick Godwin is anointed of the Lord to shake us out of our religious traditions and bring the power of the Word back into focus."

Casey Treat, pastor
Christian Faith Center